Alaska Cruising and Adventure Guide

Smooth Sailing for New and Experienced Cruisers with Stress-Free Planning, Ideal Shore Days, and Essential Travel Insights

Ocean Breeze Adventures

Copyright © 2025 by Ocean Breeze Adventures. **All rights reserved.**

The content within this book may not be reproduced, duplicated, or transmitted without direct written permission from the author or publisher.

Under no circumstances will any blame or legal responsibility be held against the publisher or author for any damages, reparations, or monetary losses due to the information contained within this book. Either directly or indirectly. You are responsible for your own choices, actions, and results.

Legal Notice:

This book is copyright-protected. This book is only for personal use. You cannot amend, distribute, sell, use, quote, or paraphrase any part of the content within this book without the consent of the author or publisher.

Disclaimer Notice:

Please note that the information contained within this document is for educational and entertainment purposes only. All effort has been expended to present accurate, up-to-date, reliable, and complete information. No warranties of any kind are declared or implied. Readers acknowledge that the author is not engaging in the rendering of legal, financial, medical, or professional advice. The content within this book has been derived from various sources. Please consult a licensed professional before attempting any techniques outlined in this book.

By reading this document, the reader agrees that under no circumstances is the author responsible for any losses, direct or indirect, which are incurred as a result of the use of the information contained within this document, including, but not limited to, errors, omissions, or inaccuracies.

Dedication

To my wife, who always has my back and makes every day an adventure.

To my son, Davey, I miss you every day and know you are with me always.

Contents

Custom Itineraries and Interactive Maps ... 1

1. Introduction to the Cruising Alaska ... 3
2. Planning Your Alaskan Adventure ... 5
3. Choosing the Right Cruise Line ... 12
4. Accessible in Alaska ... 19
5. Understanding Alaskan Culture and History ... 24
6. Wildlife and Nature Exploration ... 33
7. Adventure Activities for the Daring ... 43
8. The Inside Passage Experience ... 53
9. Voices from the Voyage ... 61
10. Immersive Experiences: From Wilderness to Wellness ... 62
11. Culinary Delights of Alaska ... 71
12. Environmental Stewardship and Eco-Friendly Travel ... 78
13. Navigating Weather and Terrain ... 86
14. Transportation and Logistics Simplified ... 94
15. Photography and Capturing Memories ... 102
16. Preparing for Safety and Emergencies ... 111
17. Sailing Away ... 120

18. Voices from the Voyage	122
Check Out this Adventure, Hawaii!	123
Praise for Ocean Breeze Adventures	126
Also by Ocean Breeze Adventures	128
About Ocean Breeze Adventures	129

Custom Itineraries and Interactive Maps

Enhancing Your Alaskan Experience

Planning your time in Alaska can feel overwhelming—where do you even start? How about with a **curated itinerary designed just for you?** Whether you're an adrenaline-seeking adventurer or looking for family-friendly fun, these itineraries ensure you make the most of every moment. From **iconic hikes and cultural landmarks to thrilling excursions and unforgettable dining**, each itinerary is carefully crafted to balance excitement and relaxation.

Inner Passage

Unlock Your Map

To make your trip even smoother, I've created interactive Google Maps to pair with your itinerary. Your first map is here, giving you access to a fully interactive guide to the Alaskan cruise ports and their surrounding adventures.

For the ultimate Alaskan experience, you can upgrade to the full Cruising Alaska map, which includes stops in Victoria, Canada; Sitka; and Seattle, WA, packed with even more features, including Glacier Bay. This expanded map makes planning effortless, with must-see locations, dining recommendations, and top activities across—all available for free when you sign up with your email.

By signing up, you'll also become part of the **Ocean Breeze Adventures community**, where you'll receive **exclusive travel tips, insider recommendations, and updates on new itineraries and travel guides**. No spam—just valuable insights to help you plan unforgettable trips.

How to Use Your Interactive Map

The maps are organized into layers: cultural stops, water adventures, land adventures, must-try eateries, recommended places to stay for all budgets, places to rent cars and accessibility items, and special OceanBreezeAdventures. Toggle the layers on or off to focus on what interests you most.

Tap on any pin for detailed descriptions, helpful links, and real-time directions in Google Maps.

To access the map throughout your trip, save it to your Google Maps account by tapping the **"Star" icon.**

Bringing Itineraries and Maps Together

Pairing these itineraries with the interactive map allows you to customize your Alaska cruise adventure based on your preferences, ports of call, and available time. Spending the morning marveling at Glacier Bay National Park and want a nearby excursion? The map will guide you to a scenic boat tour or a wildlife viewing experience in Juneau. Planning a high-adrenaline adventure? Use the map to find your next thrill, whether it's dog sledding on Mendenhall Glacier, riding the White Pass & Yukon Route Railway in Skagway, or ziplining through the treetops in Ketchikan.

This combination of pre-planned itineraries and a fully interactive map ensures that your adventure is stress-free, fun, and filled with unforgettable moments.

Ready to unlock the full Alaskan Experience map?

Simply scan the QR code and fill out the email signup form to receive instant access—and stay connected with Ocean Breeze Adventures for the best travel tips and insights!

Chapter One

Introduction to the Cruising Alaska

Bracing Alaskan air swirls across the deck of your cruise ship. Icebergs float by, glittering in the soft light of the northern sun. A glacier cracks in the distance, sounding like a faraway thunderclap. Towering peaks covered in snow seemingly reach to the horizon, their majesty accentuated by an expansive sky. Bald eagles fly above, and perhaps a whale will breach, taking your breath away. This is Alaska—wild, majestic, and waiting to be experienced.

This book will be your guide through it all, for first-time cruisers and seasoned adventurers alike. It was created to help you plan an Alaska cruise of a lifetime and will assist anyone in navigating the myriad options of every cruise line and route in the 49th state. Alaska has something for everyone, and this guide is here to help make sure you experience the best of it.

My goal in writing this book is twofold: to help you plan your trip with as little stress as possible and to inspire you to travel so that you return home not just with stories of your adventures, but also having grown as a person through your experience. Within these pages, you will find stress-free itineraries, helpful travel tips, and valuable insights about this special place that will inspire you to plan your own travels there.

I know what you need. You want smooth planning and unique discovery. You want to understand a new culture and feel like a true explorer. You might feel a bit burdened by the myriad choices, the details, the sheer volume of planning such a trip requires. This guide is about making your dream Alaskan cruise a reality, without the logistical nightmare.

I am a travel advisor, and I love to help people make the most of their travel dreams. I have been in the business for quite some time, and I truly know my way around a cruise ship and how to make it an amazing experience for you. I would love to help you make the most of your travels. Think of me as your travel BFF, and let's do this together and have a lot of fun!

What's inside this book? Real advice, step-by-step itineraries, and insider travel guidance that only someone who's been where you are can offer. We'll tell you the most rewarding shore excursions and must-see stops—the spots that only locals know about. With us, you'll never have to deal with pain points again. We'll make sure you'll never have to ask, "Is this all there is?"

The book is organized so that it takes you through every stage of your journey. Each chapter builds on the one before and takes you from how to plan a cruise, to how to enjoy your time on shore, what to pack, and when to see the northern lights. By the end of it, you'll have a complete travel guide in your hands.

I hope you will read this book with a spirit of discovery. Alaska is a place like no other, and planning your travel is part of the adventure. As you turn each page, you'll begin to feel the tug of your bowstring and the thrill of planning your voyage to these wild and wonderful places.

Thus, your invitation. Go forth and read these chapters, and start booking your Alaskan cruise. Alaska is calling, and you're invited.

Chapter Two

Planning Your Alaskan Adventure

A t the threshold of an adventure that may take you along glaciers, among wildlife, to endless horizons, there is a tingle of anticipation at just the thought of all the possibilities an Alaska cruise can entail.

Have you ever experienced that sense of adventure and discovery when making a trip plan? That feeling that may lead you to research, lists, and itineraries? The landscapes and cultures of Alaska are so animating and expansive that planning a cruise can be an adventure in itself.

It's not just a matter of choosing the route or the ship; it's about carving out an experience that resonates with who you are and what you need. Does the call of the wild resonate with you? Or perhaps a quiet coastal view? Each cruise design paints a different picture of this vast land. Let's make these choices together and plot a course for an unforgettable journey.

Choosing the Perfect Cruise Itinerary

Cruises in Alaska run the gamut from the cultural and historic Inside Passage to the wild and scenic coastline of the Gulf of Alaska. The Inside Passage is synonymous with scenic beauty—the route is an undulating succession of misty fjords and pretty bays, with coastal forests that breathe life into the landscape, and a multitude of port towns and cities.

Juneau, Skagway, and Ketchikan are almost mandatory stops, as is the Glacier Bay National Park, but you'll also find yourself passing through smaller, lesser-known destinations. Some itineraries reach as far north as the Canadian-owned islands of the Queen Charlotte Archipelago. This is a great option for those who like to allow the world to drift by—those who want a cruise where you can take a day (or two) to explore a cultural hub or sit down with some of the best natural views anywhere in the United States.

The Gulf of Alaska (a route between Vancouver or Seattle and Anchorage) is a route for those who like a bit more action: where the scenery is stunning, but you want a healthy dose of land-based adventure. It is a good option for those who are keen to experience a little of Alaska's interior as well. Stops include Hubbard Glacier and the College Fjord.

If you're an adventurous traveler, an expedition cruise on a small ship is a great choice because you can get up close to everything without the intrusiveness of a larger ship. Small ships can often navigate into areas large ships cannot, and you can truly feel like you're among nature. Imagine kayaking with sea otters or hiking through previously untouched wilderness.

A final factor that will affect your experience is whether you travel on a small or large ship. Small ships will be more personalized, often with a flexible itinerary that includes unique activities and excursions. Large ships, on the other hand, come equipped with a wide variety of amenities, entertainment, and socializing opportunities. If you are an outgoing traveler who loves meeting people, then the onboard social life of a large ship can be a lot of fun.

When picking a cruise based on personal interests, think about what you are most passionate about. Animal lovers may want to pick itineraries that offer the best chances of seeing whales, bears, and eagles. Culture and history fans may want itineraries that visit indigenous communities and historic sites. Adventure junkies will find itineraries with lots of options for hiking, kayaking, and more, so that every day brings a new thrill.

There are also seasonal variations to consider. The Northern Lights are visible from late August until late April—March being the best month—in places such as Fairbanks and Coldfoot. Whale watching is at its peak in summer, from May to September, in Juneau and Icy Strait. Your season of choice will dictate your experience, from the wildlife you come across to the weather you can enjoy.

Flexibility in your travel plans can be the difference between a great trip and a fantastic one. Alaska weather is notoriously fickle, and if you've got a long list of optional excursions and add-ons, you'll likely choose to take advantage of a good weather day.

Perhaps you can squeeze in a last-minute hike or find a tour that's just opened up. Knowing your cancellation policies will help to alleviate tensions and give you room to make adjustments, should they become necessary. Flexibility can transform your Alaskan experience from a simple trip to a collection of memorable moments.

Budgeting for Your Alaskan Adventure

The adventure starts with your cruise ticket. The cost depends on what kind of voyage you want, for how long, and what type of cabin you prefer. Cruises generally run between $600 and $5,000 per person, depending on how you customize your experience. Port fees are often a part of this.

Excursions are the next line item in your budget. They can be a city tour for under $75 or the helicopter dog sledding circuit that is up to $600. You might go on one, you might go on them all—they add up, as do dinners and drinks onboard.

Gratuities are generally expected. These are always your choice, but they show appreciation for the crew who keep your experience smooth and seamless.

You can save without compromising the experience. Fly to Alaska in the off-season, when fares are lower but the views remain sublime. Make a reservation for an early bird dinner deal at the nicest restaurant in town. Secure a bargain package deal that includes an excursion, offering the convenience of a guided tour and value for your hard-earned dollars. Book an interior cabin that lacks an ocean view but costs much less, freeing up your budget for adventures ashore.

It is tempting to skip the travel insurance, but that is your safety net. Trip cancellation/interruption insurance covers the unexpected, from canceled vacations to medical emergencies that can turn a dream trip into a nightmare and leave you out of pocket. If you must cancel, trip cancellation insurance will reimburse you.

Just as learning the local language before heading to a new country will make your stay easier and more enjoyable, knowing about currency and payment in Alaska will make your financial interactions a breeze. Credit cards are the way to go and help you avoid handling cash, but having some cash on you is a good idea, especially if you plan to shop at smaller vendors or tip service providers.

A 15–20% tip in restaurants is standard. For porters, consider giving $1–$2 per bag. These small gestures can make a big difference in showing appreciation for the hospitality you receive during your adventure.

Budgeting for Alaska is about finding that sweet spot between dreams and reality. The epic vistas, wildlife encounters, and cultural experiences are all worth it, and you can enjoy them with your budget in mind. Remember: it's about experiences, not expenses—it's about investing in memories, not just spending money.

Essential Packing Lists for Alaska's Weather

Packing for Alaska is like preparing for a multi-course meal, where each course calls for its own ingredients and preparation. Alaska's weather is as fickle as it is varied, ranging from bright and sunny to cool and drizzly. The key is layering up.

- **Base Layers:** These should be made of synthetic material that wicks away moisture, keeping your skin dry. Think thermal tops and leggings.

- **Mid Layers:** Add fleeces or wool sweaters for warmth.

- **Outer Layers:** A waterproof jacket protects against rain and wind. This combination allows you to adapt to changing temperatures without being too hot or cold.

If you plan on venturing beyond the cruise ship, specialty gear is essential. Binoculars bring distant wildlife into focus, while sturdy hiking boots provide support on rugged trails. Since cruises often alternate casual days with formal evenings, don't forget to pack dressy outfits for dinner and shows onboard.

Efficiency is key when fitting everything into your suitcase. Rolling clothes instead of folding can save space and reduce wrinkles. Packing cubes help organize your belongings into categories, making it easy to locate items without rummaging through your entire bag. Be mindful of luggage restrictions, as every inch of space counts.

Don't forget your **documentation**: passport, visas, cruise tickets, and travel insurance documents should be in your carry-on for easy access. A little organization goes a long way in avoiding last-minute stress.

Navigating Alaskan Transportation Options

If you want to get to the heart of what makes Alaska unique, you have to see it with an Alaskan perspective, and that means hopping in a bush plane, a small aircraft that opens up the vast wilderness of Alaska like a book. A bush plane takes you to places that are difficult to reach by road or boat, or where there is no road or boat access. If you want to get to an isolated lodge or explore a remote wildlife habitat, you'll likely fly into it. This is not just a means of transportation. The plane itself is part of the experience. It offers you a bird's-eye view of the rugged Alaskan landscape that few people ever see.

Railroad

The Alaska Railroad is another great way to see the state, taking you through some of the most beautiful landscapes in the entire region. From rolling past Denali's colossal peaks to winding along the coast with views of the Turnagain Arm, trains are great for relaxing into the adventure; you don't have to be the one navigating and can just drink in the views.

Ferries

Those more inclined to the sea can take advantage of the Alaska Marine Highway ferry system, connecting coastline communities in a slower, more contemplative travel experience. With a network of ferries that allow you to bring your car or RV, you can road trip through the state, stopping at various islands along the way, each with its own unique charm.

Bush Planes

Many sites allow you to book your seat on a bush plane or your train ticket online. Seasonal schedules can affect when trains run, so it's wise to look up these schedules in advance, ensuring you get to see and do all the things you're most excited about. Once you know the best times to travel, you can avoid tourist crowds by planning your trip accordingly.

You'll need to rely on local transit to get around once you're on land. Some ports have shuttles that bring you to town or a popular attraction, so by the time you're off the ship, you can start your onshore adventure. If you prefer your own pace, renting a car gives you freedom to pull over and stare at a view as long as you want—or park and wander a trailhead. It's the mix of guided tours and independent exploration that makes a trip your own.

Accessible Travel

Accessibility is always a factor in travel plans, and in Alaska, that is no different. While not all of Alaska is easily accessible—and some of the remotest places remain a challenge—the transportation systems that bring people to those places are changing for the better. The Alaska Marine Highway System, or ferry system, has been upgrading its vessels to be ADA-compliant. The Alaska Railroad has also upgraded its facilities and trains to allow greater access for people with disabilities. Many transportation providers offer services for travelers with disabilities, helping to make Alaska as accessible as possible. Accessibility will be covered in length in the next chapter.

Transportation in Alaska is often all about the getting there. Flying, riding the rails, or rolling over the glass-smooth surface of the ocean—each mode offers an experience as much about the destination as the journey. It's about finding a path that fills you with excitement, that sparks the fire in your gut, that allows you to engage in full-body travel. Your arrival is the moment you've been waiting for. But it's not the only moment you've been waiting for. In choosing how to get here, you were picking a path—a journey of adventure, story, and experience. In Alaska, transport is part of the magic.

Chapter Three

Choosing the Right Cruise Line

Alaska provides numerous travel options and diverse excursions for visitors to explore. Multiple cruise lines offer incredible journeys through Alaska. This chapter analyzes the advantages and disadvantages of each cruise line to help you select the best company for your journey.

Any travel group interested in viewing the northern lights, a solo adventurer eager to try dog sledding, or individuals requiring wheelchair access can find their ideal cruise line option.

Choosing the Right Alaska Cruise

Understanding the unique features of Alaska cruises helps before choosing specific cruise lines.

Factors to Evaluate When Picking a Cruise Line

- **Ship Size & Style:** Large ships provide numerous amenities and entertainment options, while small ships deliver intimate experiences and access to remote locations.

- **Itinerary & Ports of Call:** Some cruise lines visit major urban centers such as **Juneau, Ketchikan, and Skagway,** while others explore less frequented locations including **Wrangell and Sitka.**

- **Glacier Viewing Opportunities:** Some itineraries feature **Glacier Bay National Park,** while others highlight **Hubbard Glacier or Tracy Arm Fjord.**

- **Onboard Experience:** Different cruise lines create unique atmospheres, ranging from adventure-focused to luxury-based settings.

- **Accessibility & Special Accommodations:** Cruise lines vary in their accessibility features, so travelers with mobility, hearing, or vision impairments need to evaluate each option before booking.

Major Cruise Lines That Sail to Alaska

Several cruise lines offer exceptional journeys through Alaska, each with unique features and accessibility accommodations.

Norwegian Cruise Line (NCL) – Freestyle Adventure

Overview: Enjoy a flexible and laid-back cruise experience with unlimited dining options and multiple entertainment choices.

Itineraries:

- One-way sailings between Seattle, Vancouver, and Seward.
- Round-trip Seattle sailings for convenience.
- Glacier Bay inclusion on select itineraries.

Best For: Active travelers and families who prefer a casual ocean journey.

Ships & Accessibility Features:

- Norwegian Bliss, Encore, Sun, Jewel, Spirit.
- Priority boarding options.
- Accessible staterooms and tender boats on select ships.

Holland America Line—Classic Alaska

Overview: A premium cruise line specializing in cultural exploration and wildlife discovery.

Itineraries:

- Exclusive Glacier Bay permits.
- Denali land-and-sea packages for extended Alaska experiences.
- Stops at smaller ports like Sitka and Wrangell.

Best For: Mature travelers, couples, and nature enthusiasts.

Ships & Accessibility Features:

- Eurodam, Nieuw Amsterdam, Koningsdam, Westerdam.
- Large-print menus, wheelchair-accessible staterooms, and ASL interpreter services.

Princess Cruises – Glacier Exploration & Land Extensions

Overview: A leader in Alaska cruises, specializing in scenic journeys and glacier tours.

Itineraries:

- Exclusive Glacier Bay permits.

- **Denali & Canadian Rockies extensions.**

Best For: Travelers seeking luxurious onboard accommodations and in-depth exploration of Alaska.

Ships & Accessibility Features:

- Discovery Princess, Majestic Princess, Royal Princess, Grand Princess.
- Accessible public spaces, shore excursion assistance, and Braille signage.

Celebrity Cruises—Upscale Luxury & Comfort

Overview: A refined cruise experience offering state-of-the-art luxury amenities for complete relaxation.

Itineraries:

- **Small-ship feel with big-ship amenities.**
- **Glacier Bay inclusion on select itineraries.**

Best For: Couples and solo travelers who appreciate gourmet dining and luxury travel.

Ships & Accessibility Features:

- Celebrity Solstice, Celebrity Eclipse, Celebrity Millennium.
- Automatic doors, accessible staterooms, and hearing assistance equipment.

Royal Caribbean—Adventure & High-Energy Cruising

Overview: A cruise line known for **high-energy ship activities** and a family-friendly environment.

Itineraries:

- One-way & round-trip options from Seattle and Vancouver.
- Stops at Juneau, Skagway, Ketchikan, and Sitka.

Best For: Young families and active travelers looking for adventure amenities like rock climbing and surf simulators.

Ships & Accessibility Features:

- Quantum of the Seas, Ovation of the Seas, Radiance of the Seas.
- Accessible FlowRider surf simulators, accessible seating, and priority boarding.

Disney Cruise Line—Family-Friendly Adventures

Overview: Disney's Alaska cruises offer **enchanting adventures** with world-class service and entertainment.

Itineraries:

- Family-friendly Alaska excursions.
- Departures from Vancouver with stops at Juneau, Skagway, and Ketchikan.

Best For: Families, Disney fans, and travelers **seeking kid-friendly activities.**

Ships & Accessibility Features:

- Disney Wonder.
- Accessible cabins, wheelchair-friendly kids' areas, and ASL-interpreted character meet-and-greet sessions.

Small-Ship & Expedition Cruises—Off-the-Beaten-Path Exploration

For travelers seeking exclusive remote location access, small-ship cruises provide intimate, adventure-driven experiences.

- **Lindblad Expeditions/National Geographic:** Small-group excursions with expert naturalists.

- **UnCruise Adventures:** Highly immersive experiences with flexible itineraries.

- **American Cruise Lines:** Focus on small-ship comfort and exclusive ports.

Best For: Travelers who want a **personalized, off-the-grid experience.**

Unique Alaska Cruise Features & Excursions

When selecting an **Alaska cruise,** consider the distinct experiences each offers.

Scenic Glacier Viewing Experiences

- Glacier Bay National Park: Exclusive access for Holland America & Princess Cruises.

- Hubbard Glacier: A highlight on Norwegian and Celebrity itineraries.

- Tracy Arm Fjord: A magnificent glacial fjord visited by multiple cruise lines.

Wildlife Encounters

- Whale-watching excursions in Juneau.

- Bear viewing in Ketchikan.

- Bald eagle spotting in Sitka.

Adventure & Cultural Excursions

- Dog sledding on Mendenhall Glacier.

- Native Alaskan heritage tours at totem pole parks.

- White Pass & Yukon Route scenic rail rides.

Final Thoughts

Your travel style, priorities, and accessibility requirements determine the best cruise line for your Alaska voyage.

Whether you dream of a family adventure, a luxury getaway, or an immersive nature experience, Alaska cruises provide the perfect option.

The next chapter is all about making rugged Alaska open for everyone. We will cover accessibility and how to make your accessible cruise a reality.

Chapter Four

Accessible in Alaska

Experiencing Alaska on Your Terms

You find yourself standing on the ship deck as you smoothly move toward Ketchikan. The cool air envelops you while the solid weight of your wheelchair anchors your presence to the present. The distant cries of bald eagles reverberate throughout the sky. Your Alaskan adventure stands before you, ready to be experienced exactly as you choose.

Despite common misconceptions, Alaska's wild landscapes attract adventurers of all ages and abilities. This chapter will explain the main accessibility barriers and demonstrate how proper planning and resources allow people to fully experience Alaska's beauty without restrictions while making their dream vacation real.

While planning an Alaskan adventure is thrilling, it becomes complex when ensuring accessibility for all travelers. Finding a travel specialist who is educated in accessibility services is critical for planning a successful trip. Choose a travel agent certified as a Special Needs Group Advocate since they possess the necessary expertise to create a smooth travel experience.

My role as an Accessible Travel Specialist ensures your cruise runs without issues by arranging necessary accessibility accommodations and managing your mobility or medical equipment before you board and after your trip ends.

Cruise Line Accommodations

Major cruise lines such as Norwegian, Holland America, Princess, and Royal Caribbean have developed features that enable all passengers to navigate their ships with ease and comfort.

Accessible Staterooms

The design of accessible staterooms combines extra space and specific features to facilitate easier movement. These rooms typically include:

- Wider doorways to accommodate wheelchairs and scooters.
- Roll-in showers with grab bars, shower seats, and handheld showerheads for easy bathing.
- Lowered closet bars, shelves, and light switches.
- Emergency call buttons for additional peace of mind during the stay.
- Automatic door openers on select ships.

Limited availability makes early booking of these rooms essential. An Accessible Travel Specialist will help you find the stateroom that best fits your requirements.

Navigating the Ship

Cruise ships offer design features to support passengers with different abilities.

- Public areas contain ramps and broad hallways, while elevators feature Braille and audio announcements to support visually impaired passengers.

- Accessible seating options throughout theaters, lounges, and dining areas enable all passengers to participate in onboard activities and entertainment.

- Pool lifts are available on many ships for passengers who require assistance entering and leaving swimming facilities.

Cruise ships provide the convenience of renting scooters and wheelchairs, which will be delivered right to your stateroom for use during your trip.

Available Equipment Rentals

These popular equipment rentals help enhance your cruise experience by adding comfort and accessibility:

- **Scooters:** Standard, heavy-duty, and bariatric scooters ensure easy mobility. Bariatric scooters require an accessible room.

- **Wheelchairs and Powerchairs:** Standard, heavy-duty, and bariatric models exist for both manual and electric versions. Accessible rooms are required for power chairs.

- **Walkers and Rollators:** Available in standard and heavy-duty options. Walkers help maintain balance, while rollators improve movement and contain a seat for breaks.

- **Raised Toilet Seats and Shower Chairs:** Increase bathroom accessibility.

- **Hospital Beds, Bed Rails, and Reclining Chairs:** Options include hospital beds and bed rails with lifts to aid transfers in your stateroom.

- **Oxygen Concentrators and CPAP Machines:** A prescription is required for oxygen rentals, but your Accessible Travel Specialist will guide you through the process.

- **Hearing and Vision Assistance Devices:** Includes vibrating alert systems, large-print materials, Braille documents, and listening support tools.

- **Joy on the Beach (JOB) Chair:** A beach wheelchair with large wheels that smoothly moves across sandy surfaces. This chair can roll straight into the water without requiring a lifting device.

How the Rental Process Works

The equipment rental system functions with simplicity to minimize travel stress associated with heavy medical equipment.

1. Secure your cruise reservation and review your accessibility requirements.

2. Use a reliable provider like the **Special Needs Group** to book your equipment.

3. Your equipment will reach your stateroom and be prepared before you step onto the ship.

4. The rented equipment will be collected from your cabin before you leave the ship at the end of your cruise.

Enjoy your cruise with peace of mind, knowing this service allows you to travel light while providing all necessary equipment upon arrival.

Trusted Equipment Provider: Special Needs Group

The **Special Needs Group** is the top equipment rental company for cruise travelers. You can ask your Accessible Travel Specialist to assist with rentals or visit their website to reserve devices.

- **Print book users:** Scan the QR code to access the Special Needs Group website.

- **Ebook users:** Click the link to visit the Special Needs Group website.

Final Thoughts

A cruise enables all people to experience Alaska's beauty by providing unrestricted access to the region. Passengers can fully enjoy the stunning views of the **Last Frontier** through pre-booked accommodations, mobility assistance, and specialized onboard services.

This book presents accessible excursions and offers guidance on top activities and destinations for mobility-impaired travelers. At the end of each chapter, you will find recommendations for accessible adventures.

Chapter Five

Understanding Alaskan Culture and History

S tepping from your ship onto the Alaskan shore, the air vibrates with stories of the past. Anchoring in Alaska is more than exploring the raw beauty of nature—it's about experiencing a patchwork of cultures woven together with threads from ancient times, and the celebrations and life of the present. Here, the past and present pulse to the rhythm of vibrant indigenous cultures practicing traditional lifestyles that continue to shape Alaska's heritage. To truly know Alaska is to journey through its cultures that span back centuries with the Tlingit, Haida, Inupiat, Yupik, and Athabascan peoples.

The Indigenous Cultures of Alaska

Since time immemorial, the Tlingit and Haida have inhabited the lands of the towering cedars and the rocky shores and islands of the Pacific Northwest Coast. They've lived interdependently with the forest and sea for thousands of years.

Their lives and customs are rooted in the land, evident in their complex clan systems and potlatches that celebrate life transitions and cement intergenerational community ties. Totem poles can act as sentinels of history. These towering wooden sentries would have been carved to depict a family's lineage and the stories of those who came before them. Each pole is a masterpiece of fine art and storytelling. The carvings and paintings would be made with careful detail and deliberate purpose.

The Inupiat and Yupik peoples of the northern tundra live a seasonally rooted subsistence life. Everything they do, from hunting to fishing, is tied to the natural world. The Athabascans of the interior forest are known for their storytelling traditions, where elders describe what they've learned from experiences and create a history of family and community.

Language is a lifeline to culture, and in Alaska, efforts to revitalize indigenous languages are vibrant and ongoing. Language immersion schools such as Nikaitchuat Iḷisaġviat and Ayaprun Elitnaurvik are rays of hope in this effort, offering intensives that not only teach language but also values and worldviews unique to the cultures of the Iñupiaq and Yugtun peoples. These schools are key to keeping language alive and vital, so consider getting more involved in community-led revitalization work or learning a few phrases from a native speaker on your travels. These efforts to better know the cultures that you encounter can be profoundly rewarding.

Many of Alaska Natives' arts and crafts are a testament to creativity: totem pole carving, beadwork, and basket weaving are not just crafts, but cultural expressions of identity, each item the product of a maker and a culture. Purchasing their work allows you to help a community preserve these traditions. As you go shopping at local markets and galleries, think of the stories behind the pieces and the hands that fashioned them. As you leave your mark on the landscape, ethical purchasing allows you to leave your footprint on a community's spirit.

Visiting cultural centers and embarking on guided tours can also reveal ways of life and histories of these remarkable peoples. These are chances to learn directly from those who know the land best. But engage respectfully; come with an open mind and a willingness to listen and learn. Many communities welcome tourists who are genuinely interested in learning about their ways of life. Many guided tours are led by community members, who will share not just information but personal stories that bring history to life.

Historical Landmarks and Their Stories

On a walk through Alaska, you might hear the past in the trees—at least, if you listen. Perhaps at Sitka National Historical Park, one of Alaska's two national historical parks, where the forest is full of stories. Sitka National Historical Park, Alaska's first federally designated park, is located in the southern part of the state on Baranof Island, and commemorates the so-called Russian-American era, when the fur trade reigned and a few thousand Russians carved out a life among the native Tlingit.

It is the site of the Battle of Sitka, fought by Tlingit warriors who resisted the Russian invasion of their home in 1804, an event that shifted the power balance dramatically in southeastern Alaska. Museums in Sitka National Historical Park and the adjacent Sitka National Historical Park commemorate the Russians' arrival at Sitka, but they illustrate more than just the past. The totem poles in the park's totem trail are living monuments of adaptation and cultural resilience—a place where Tlingit warriors fought for their home and the Russians invaded.

The Russian Bishop's House next door was built in the 1840s and is one of the few remaining buildings from the Russian colonial era in North America. It served as the residence of the Russian Orthodox Church for many years. Tour the Bishop's House, and you'll be transported to life in the 19th century, when the house bustled with the priests and bishops who worked here to spread the Russians' influence in North America: step into the living room and imagine the conversations that took place there.

Take a few steps back, and watch in your mind's eye as your host snaps on their leather boots to go about their business. Tiptoe up the stairs and walk by the bedrooms. Imagine the men who slept in these rooms, dreaming about their work. If the walls could talk, they would share stories of the priests and bishops who worked in this house, spreading the Russians' influence in North America.

The Alaskan Gold Rush plays a part in this history as well, when prospectors flocked to the wilderness to try their fortune on gold that could be panned from the earth. Some of the stories of these times bring to mind the Wild West, when prospectors flocked to boomtowns, which popped up with saloons, supply stores, and miners overnight. This part of the history is captured in the strip mines and abandoned cabins that dot the landscape.

But history is not just about those big dates and profound changes; it is also the stories that make that past come alive. Imagine sitting with a local historian who is telling a story passed down for generations. Maybe they have a family legend about a great-grandparent who struck it rich—or lost everything—in the Gold Rush. It is there, in the details of this personal history, that the dates and facts come alive.

These stories are worth preserving because they will be passed down to the next generation, and the next, and the next. Many of these sites would not still exist if it weren't for the tireless efforts of volunteers and historical societies working behind the scenes.

You can get involved with these efforts by volunteering your time or through donations. The more you connect with the history of this great land, the more you will connect with Alaska. By being part of these preservation efforts, you become part of the story—ensuring that the history of Alaska is never lost or forgotten.

Participating Respectfully

Step into a hot community hall, the smell of burning cedar and drums filling the air, the whisper of beaded ribbons against the air as traditional dresses rustle. These workshops promised an opportunity to connect with the Alaskan traditions that have helped shape the land for thousands of years. And they lived up to expectations.

When you attend an Alaskan cultural workshop, you don't just learn a new dance or listen to a story. You feel the heartbeat of the community, the rhythm of its cadences, its beat. It is more than learning about Alaska or immersing yourself in its traditions. Every step and every gesture tell a story. Traditional dance workshops let you feel the community's pulse through time and space, from one generation to the next. Storytelling allows you to experience times and places that have long disappeared, to hear the voices of elders, and to listen to the stories that have echoed through generations in the oral traditions of the state.

All of these experiences can be profound, but to make them so, you must connect with respect. Knowing the cultural protocols demonstrates that your presence is welcome and that it is appreciated.

Simple things can help. For example, always try to observe before you participate, and dress modestly. The same goes for listening. Don't interrupt people as they tell their stories. Ask questions—but ask them respectfully. For instance, rather than opening with the question, "Do you think that...?" an opening question more willingly welcomed and respectful of cultural context might be, "Can you tell me more about how...?" Or, more open-ended again, you might ask, "How is it that...?" If you are unsure about something, ask your host.

There are workshops across Alaska that illuminate an aspect of the local heritage, each one a portal into the daily lives and traditions of the people. A native cooking class might have you wielding a cleaver and working over an open fire to make salmon or a berry-laden treat called akutaq that has been eaten for generations. Classes often delve into the stories that interweave food with cultural identity and the survival of communities through the long winters.

Classes in basket weaving and pottery-making let you work with your hands to learn techniques that can be traced back for generations. Every piece that you finish becomes a reminder of the skills and stories that your instructors have given you.

Many of these workshops' past participants don't just take away particular skills; they also take with them a sense of personal transformation and connection that they haven't felt elsewhere. A visitor to a dance workshop described how they learned more than steps; they caught sight of the people's resilience and their sense of community. Someone fresh from a storytelling session said that they felt transported into the stories and now had a new respect for the power of oral history. Such encounters transform, open eyes and hearts, and can broaden the awareness of cultural and human diversity.

Journaling Prompt

Consider a significant cultural experience you've had and how it's changed you. What did you learn about a community or a group of people? How did the experience make you feel, and how did it affect you as a person? Write about this experience and what made it so powerful, as well as what you learned about yourself in the process.

Local Traditions and Festivals

Standing on the sidelines at Alaska's festivals, you'll feel energy buzzing in the air, sweat beading on everyone's foreheads, and be close enough to smell the hickory smoke and hear voices calling in the Gambetson language or Yup'ik. These are more than fun social gatherings, more than showcases for the arts and crafts of the community. They are the heartbeat of a community, the pulse of a society that can only be understood by being part of the action.

The Iditarod Trail Sled Dog Race, a race of endurance for both mushers and dogs, has become an icon for all the festivals. It is held each March, with teams racing for 1,100 miles, from Anchorage northwest to Nome, retracing the Iditarod Trail once used for mail and supply deliveries via dog sled teams. Crowds of fans show up, cheering on teams to see if their favorite can take the lead. Spectators come to the starting line in Willow, Alaska, about 50 miles northwest of Anchorage. They watch as mushers and their dog teams race off the starting line at the beginning of the Iditarod Trail Sled Dog Race.

An equally meaningful ritual is the Alaska State Fair, held at the end of summer in Palmer, a small town located 40 miles northeast of Anchorage. Locals and visitors from around the world flock to the fair, where they mingle together to celebrate agriculture, crafts, and the arts. Adjacent to the vast, red-and-white commercial and livestock buildings are colorful booths brimming with giant vegetables, vibrant flower arrangements, and intricate handiwork. You can sample everything from reindeer sausage to fresh salmon caught that day, while listening to music and watching kids enjoy carnival rides.

The state fair isn't just a commercial venture but a celebration of what Alaskans produce and the communities they live in.

Other celebrations of Alaska Native cultures are more explicitly political. Every two years, Juneau plays host to Celebration, a festival that honors the Tlingit, Haida, and Tsimshian cultures and tribes. This gathering of dance, spectacle, and storytelling is an assertion of indigenous pride. The streets fill with the thrum of drums and the jangle of leather and feathers as dancers in regalia perform for a crowd that spills out of the ornately carved totem poles lining the promenade and into the bustling bars and restaurants down the block.

The festival is a powerful moment of solidarity and cultural affirmation—a reminder to outsiders that there are many ways to live and many peoples who have long called Alaska home.

These festivals aren't just dates on a calendar but essential expressions of identity and community, manifestations of the past in the present, and of tradition's role in giving shape to Alaskan life. By attending them, you become an insider to what it means to be Alaskan, and you will feel attached to the land and its people in a far more profound way. These festivals are about life and tradition and what is passed down from one generation to the next.

There are a few things to keep in mind when planning to attend these festivals. For the Iditarod, the best places to watch are at the start in Anchorage or along the trail at the checkpoints where the teams are. Make sure to dress warmly—the temperatures can be brutal—and bring along some extra clothes to deal with the varying weather. Also, expect crowds.

The Alaska State Fair is held from late August to early September, and the weather can range from hot to cold, so you'll want to bring layers of clothing to deal with the fluctuating temperatures. The fairgrounds are large, so bring comfortable shoes and be prepared to walk a lot. Celebration is informal, but when attending a powwow or gathering, consult locals about the best places to watch the events and listen to the stories they have to tell.

While it might be tempting to document photographs of every moment, it is important to be mindful of the cultural sensitivity of these events. Ask for permission before taking photographs, especially in the case of indigenous performances. Remember that certain moments might be sacred. You can also show respect by patronizing local vendors and artisans. Buying handmade crafts or local produce not only helps to bolster the local economy but also gives you a keepsake to remember your time spent in Alaska.

Final Thoughts

Life in all its forms is on vivid display in Alaska's festivals, from the hardscrabble resilience of the Iditarod to the youthful exuberance of the State Fair and the communal pride of Celebration. You're invited, at each one, to become part of the narrative of Alaska at its very best, a narrative in which the past and present come together in a dance. These festivals give you a glimpse of Alaska's cultural landscape, the better to prepare you for the wonders that await.

Exploring Alaska's Cultural Heritage with Accessibility in Mind

Alaska's rich cultural heritage is open to all, and many historical sites, museums, and events are becoming more accessible to travelers with mobility, sensory, or other needs. For historical sites such as Sitka National Historical Park, accessible trails are available, but some areas may include uneven terrain—checking with visitor centers for wheelchair-friendly routes is recommended. The Russian Bishop's House offers a guided tour, but upper floors are accessible only by stairs; those with mobility challenges may prefer exploring the lower levels and exhibits.

For festivals and cultural workshops, planning ahead ensures a comfortable experience. The Alaska State Fairgrounds are large and require significant walking, but wheelchair rentals, accessible seating, and rest areas are available. At Celebration in Juneau, parades and performances can get crowded, so early arrival ensures the best vantage point. The Iditarod Trail Sled Dog Race is held in extreme winter conditions, making accessibility challenging at some checkpoints, but viewing locations in Anchorage and Nome provide accessible spectator areas.

For immersive experiences such as native storytelling, dance performances, and workshops, most venues are designed to accommodate all visitors. Traditional workshops often take place in community centers or cultural institutions, which generally provide accessible seating and facilities. Visitors with sensory sensitivities may want to check ahead regarding lighting, sound levels, and crowd sizes at performance events.

Travelers can enhance their experience by contacting local visitor centers, festival organizers, or accessibility coordinators in advance to arrange accommodations, transportation, and seating assistance where needed. By planning ahead, all visitors can fully embrace Alaska's vibrant cultures and traditions in a way that best suits their needs.

Chapter Six

Wildlife and Nature Exploration

Standing near the rim of a big, flat bowl of an open field in Denali National Park, the cool, clean morning air is crisp against your skin as the dawn sun edges its way up over the high peaks. The ground is hard, the air is quiet save for the distant call of a raven, and then, suddenly, movement: it's a mother bear and her cubs venturing into the world for the first time this spring, stepping out of their winter den.

It is spring in Alaska.

And springtime in Alaska is a miracle, when the season awakens the land and brings a riot of wild things to life. Timing is everything for witnessing the spectacles of nature.

The awakening of bears in the spring is my favorite season in Alaska. In Denali National Park, it is a time of wonder as grizzly bears emerge from their winter slumber and begin to feed on the new growth. It's a special time to be on the trails in the park, as you never know when you might turn a corner and come face to face with one of these magnificent animals.

However, bears are not the only stars that return in the spring. Bowhead whales begin their migration up the coast at the same time, while migratory songbirds return to the skies. The land and sea tango.

Magical in a whole other way is summer's drama of predator and prey. Along streams, salmon leap madly upstream, while bears gather along the shores, catching the offerings and taking their meal back into the woods, as eagles circle overhead, their eyes sharp in the sky. It's a drama of predator and prey that plays out in places such as Katmai National Park, where the Brooks River is alive with activity.

The Inside Passage lures sightseers looking for whales. Humpbacks and orcas put on performances that live on in memory for a lifetime.

The seasons in Alaska drive behavior and, ultimately, the movements of wildlife. Birds migrate, capitalizing on atmospheric shifts to travel thousands of miles between warmer and cooler climates. Bears hibernate as they head into winter, their activity dictated by the seasons. Knowing this adds richness to a trip, giving you insight into the best times of year to visit for the best wildlife encounters.

Fall is when caribou migrate, herds moving toward winter ranges as if they were creating a living tapestry across the tundra. It's then that you get to see nature in motion, to appreciate the way this place works.

Logistical planning is important. Booking guided tours with reputable operators can help you to make the most of your wildlife-viewing adventure; they'll lead you to prime locations and, perhaps equally important, provide you with a knowledgeable guide who understands which animals are active when, the adaptations wild animals have to their habitats, and so on. You'll want to book well in advance, particularly if you're visiting during peak seasons.

Consider operators such as Katmai Wilderness Lodge, where bear-viewing is intimate, or Kenai Fjords Tours, offering a chance to see the marine landscapes brimming with life. These tours will maximize your chances of memorable wildlife encounters while also making sure your adventure is done safely and responsibly.

Wildlife Viewing Checklist

- **Best Times to Go:** Spring for bear emergence in Denali; summer for whale-watching in the Inside Passage.

- **Prime Locations:** Katmai National Park for bears; Kenai Fjords for marine life.

- **Tour Operators:** Katmai Wilderness Lodge, Kenai Fjords Tours.

- **Seasonal Considerations:** Plan around migratory patterns and hibernation periods.

Wild Alaska is a means to engage with a landscape that is as wild as the animals that live there. Every season brings its own spectacles. In spring, baby blue whales and gray whales make their way north into the Bering and Chukchi seas. Bowhead whales haul out of their wintering grounds in the Bering Strait to breed in the pack ice of the Chukchi Sea. In the summer, the first brown bears with cubs emerge from their dens. In early autumn, wolves begin their autumnal migrations.

Porpoises, humpback whales, orcas, sperm whales, fin whales, minke whales, and even the elusive right whale are all spotted during the feeding frenzy of the fall and winter.

Ethical and Responsible Wildlife Observation

Watching wildlife in Alaska can elicit a powerful sense of connection with nature. At the same time, this privilege requires a commitment to observing ethically. Safe distances are the norm for observing wild animals in order to avoid disturbing them. Bears and moose can be fascinating to watch, but they will react badly if you get too close.

You should keep at least 300 feet from bears and 100 feet from moose if you want them to feel comfortable and be safe. Keeping a safe distance respects their space and, consequently, yours. Binoculars and scopes are your friends if you want to get up close and personal with wildlife. They allow you to see animals in all their spectacular detail without crossing the invisible boundary that protects both them and you.

The Leave No Trace principles are more than just suggestions; they are a promise to keep Alaska's wild places as pristine as possible. When you pick up all your garbage, you make a small yet meaningful effort to guarantee that, no matter how you found this spot, you are leaving it as you found it. When you stay on trails that have likely been placed in spaces where human traffic can do the least damage to a fragile ecosystem, you are committing to not tromping your way through an area that may be eagerly awaiting your arrival. Those trails may have been carefully placed to lead you through the landscape while protecting as much of the ecosystem as possible. You can leave knowing that you have had a hand in keeping this place the way it was before you arrived.

Education, then, should lie at the core of ethical wildlife observation. As you learn about the species you are observing and their ecosystems, you cannot help but develop greater respect and understanding. Signing up for a wildlife education program can lead to useful insights into the lives of animals and the delicate connections between species.

Many parks and reserves run guided tours that incorporate didactic components. Reading about local ecosystems before you venture out can also help you to appreciate the complex web of life you're about to witness. These resources provide context, turning an otherwise routine sighting into a "teachable moment" that links you to the natural world.

Picture, instead, a guided tour in Kenai Fjords National Park, with a ranger escort who provides context for a group of sea otters. The tour participants look on from a respectful distance, using binoculars to observe the otters' playful antics without causing them stress. Responsible wildlife viewing can be an exciting, engaging, and worthwhile experience.

Conservation success stories are another reason wildlife-watching is worthwhile. A growing number of species populations are being successfully restored thanks to responsible wildlife practices.

In Alaska, the bald eagle population, once nearly wiped out, is now thriving. Not long ago, it was illegal to view or photograph bald eagles; they were such a rare sight. However, thanks to a combination of habitat restoration and responsible wildlife practices, today the bald eagle is seen as a symbol of strength and possibility.

Wildlife Ethics Reflection

- Think back to a time when you encountered wild animals in their natural habitats.

- How did you feel during the experience?

- What did you do to minimize your impact on the animals and their environment?

- How might Leave No Trace principles guide your future wildlife observations?

- How would education foster your connection to and appreciation for the natural world?

With each sighting, you become part of a bigger effort to promote conservation and to ensure respect for the natural world. Ethical wildlife watching is not just a practice—it is a form of reverence to the amazing beings that share this planet with us.

By maintaining your distance, following Leave No Trace principles, and keeping your knowledge constantly updated, you are part of a legacy of guardianship that will ensure that wild places continue to exist and thrive for generations to come.

Navigating the Tidewater Glaciers

Imagine standing at the edge of a tidewater glacier where the ancient ice meets the ocean in an ever-shifting tapestry of raw power and natural beauty. These glaciers, with their towering ice cliffs and elaborate patterns, are not just frozen rivers. They are integral parts of Alaska's ecosystems.

Watch as a giant iceberg chunk splits off with a crack and plunges into the ocean in an event that sends ripples through the bay. This natural phenomenon is not just a spectacle but an ecological event. Nutrients spill into the sea, triggering plankton blooms and inspiring feeding frenzies of fish, whales, and seabirds.

The cold, nutrient-rich waters spark a sea of life and ecosystem richness that sustains and supports a diverse array of species in the marine environment. This is the story of glaciers: the builders of the landscape, shaping valleys and fjords over millennia and holding the fossil record of the Earth's geological history.

Hiking on its surface or cruising through its icy waters by boat, it's important to respect the environment and be prepared. The landscape can be hazardous and unpredictable, with hundreds of meters of the glacier collapsing beneath you into deep crevasses. In most places, you slip and slide across the surface, and so crampons are generally necessary to be able to walk, with layers of clothes to keep you warm and a good walking stick to add balance.

To tackle a glacier for the first time, many people have a guide take them through it. Glacier hiking can be a challenging experience, and many people feel safer being guided by someone who has been there before and knows how to get you to safety. Guides not only protect you from dangers but also provide information about the glacier itself and the ecosystem around it, creating the possibility for a unique tailor-made adventure.

The glaciers are not static: they're always in flux, and climate change is speeding up that flux. The retreat of these vast accumulations of ice is a tangible sign of a warming world. Melting glaciers contribute to rising seas, which can alter coastline habitats and communities. Retreating glaciers also change the physical landscape, which can affect the ecosystems that depend on cold, stable conditions. Ongoing conservation efforts involve studying these changes and mitigating their impacts. Scientists are scrambling to understand what a warming world means and how to respond. Supporting these efforts—whether through awareness or action—is one of the ways we can protect such places for future generations.

Some of the most accessible and picturesque tidewater glaciers in Alaska are found at Exit Glacier in Kenai Fjords National Park, a popular destination for tourists viewing its majestic tongue (the portion of a glacier extending down into a valley) and surrounding vista. A series of hiking trails follows the glacier to its edge, affording visitors safe vantage points from which the glacier's intricate formations can be viewed up close.

Hubbard Glacier, near the community of Yakutat, is one of the largest tidewater glaciers in North America and is another must-see. It is known for calving events that routinely occur, keeping observers in awe of nature's power, watching the glacier's edge crumble into the sea.

You become a part of something greater, a witness to the geological processes that sculpted our planet over eons. Stand on a glacier, and you are in tune with the seasons, standing in the temporal space that glaciers inhabit. A place to ponder the past and contemplate the future, to embrace the fragility of these frozen places, and the need to protect them. The glacier is the destination and the journey, a place to explore, learn, and inspire.

Birdwatching Hotspots and Tips

The first thing my wife and I did after moving to Alaska was birdwatching, and we haven't stopped. Lurking in this far northern destination are some of the most wondrous avian spectacles in the world. At the Copper River Delta, where the air is filled with birdsong and the clatter of millions of shorebirds winging north in the spring. It's a bird's paradise, a wetland teeming with life that serves as a crucial stopover for birds migrating along the Pacific Flyway. You can watch Western Sandpipers and Dunlins rising and falling in unison, their wings smacking silver in the sunlight. The Delta becomes a whirling canvas of wave and sound—a choreographed display that is simultaneously humbling and exhilarating.

Instead, Potter Marsh in Anchorage is an oasis of calm. This lush marsh is a gem of a place, the best repository in town when it comes to waterfowl diversity, and a popular destination for anyone—native or visitor—who wants a nature break.

The soft, reedy sound of the marsh envelops you as you walk the boardwalks, the individual songs of hidden birds woven into a musical tapestry. Potter Marsh is at its best in the early morning and late afternoon, when the light is soft, and the birds are busy. Here you might see a sleek Northern Pintail, or you might see the bright colors of the Wood Duck, each a small wonder, another gem to add to the mix.

If you are keen to identify the birds of Alaska, birding apps can become your best friends as you travel along the highways, riding in a rental car or bus, with their audio databases and visual identifications of every bird. Matched with your findings, your journey can become a learning experience.

Knowing when the best times to watch are is important: it's best during dawn and dusk. That is when you have the greatest chance of hearing and seeing a bird come alive. The birds are most visible in the low light of early morning and late evening—not only because they are moving around at that time but also because the low angle of the sun adds a golden hue to the shadows and light, making everything more beautiful.

Alaska is home to a handful of unique and hard-to-see species that are there largely to offer the thrill of discovery to any birder who decides to bird the state. These include the Kittlitz's Murrelet, a diminutive little seabird that nests in the remote, nippy reaches of Alaska's coast, and the Spectacled Eider, a handsome duck that's a favorite among birders due to its showy plumage and some particularly odd behavior. Seen or not, birding these species is always a joy, teaching the birdwatcher just a little bit more about the secret corners of Alaska's wild places.

Ethical birdwatching involves respecting those habitats, not disturbing the animals or plants that live there, and minimizing your impact by staying out of nesting areas during the breeding season. Many breeding birds abandon their nests when they are disturbed or lay eggs that hatch late and have less chance of survival.

Silence is another basic principle. Being quiet and moving slowly means you will be out there longer, and the birds are more likely to reveal themselves. That's the point: seeing the birds in the wild, behaving naturally, is what makes it so special.

Final Thoughts

As you explore Alaska's birding hotspots, remember that each sighting is a reminder of the intricate web of life that defines this extraordinary land. From the bustling Copper River Delta to the peaceful Potter Marsh, each location offers a unique window into the avian world. Equipped with knowledge, respect, and a sense of wonder, your birdwatching adventures in Alaska will not only enrich your understanding of these remarkable creatures but also deepen your appreciation for the natural world. With every bird you spot, you're not just observing—you're participating in a timeless tradition of discovery and respect for nature.

Experiencing Alaska's Wildlife & Natural Wonders with Accessibility in Mind

Alaska's wildlife encounters and natural wonders are among the most breathtaking in the world, and many locations offer accessible options for travelers with mobility or sensory needs. For bear-viewing in Denali National Park and Katmai National Park, guided tours with transportation can help visitors avoid difficult trails and rugged terrain. Some tour companies provide accessible vehicles or boat-based bear-watching experiences for a more comfortable, close-up view of these incredible animals.

Whale-watching in the Inside Passage is one of the most accessible wildlife activities, as many cruise ships and tour boats offer wheelchair-friendly viewing decks, ramps, and accessible restrooms. Motion-sensitive travelers may wish to prepare for potential seasickness, as ocean conditions can vary.

For those wanting to witness tidewater glaciers, boat tours to Hubbard Glacier and Kenai Fjords offer some of the best viewing opportunities without the need for physically demanding excursions. Glacier hiking, however, requires significant mobility, balance, and cold-weather gear. Travelers who prefer a stable experience can opt for boat-based glacier viewing or accessible boardwalks at Exit Glacier in Kenai Fjords National Park.

Birdwatching locations like Potter Marsh in Anchorage are wheelchair-friendly with accessible boardwalks that allow for excellent viewing opportunities without the need for strenuous walking. Remote birding spots like Copper River Delta require guided transportation or specialized access.

By planning ahead and choosing the right guided tours, boat-based excursions, or accessible boardwalks, Alaska's stunning wildlife and landscapes remain open to everyone, regardless of physical ability. Whether it's watching whales from a ship, viewing bears from a comfortable observation area, or listening to migratory birds in a peaceful marsh, Alaska's natural wonders can be enjoyed by all.

Chapter Seven

Adventure Activities for the Daring

You slowly paddle your kayak among sheer cliffs amid the distant din of waterfalls in an Alaskan fjord. You're in crisp air, with mist down low over the water. You're part of the scene, moving to the pull of the tide. A sea otter skims by and looks at you before diving with a splash. This is the appeal of paddling Alaska's fjords—a connection with nature that's as tranquil as it is adventurous.

Awe-inspiring fjords of misty Alaska are stunning, a geological and natural landscape of dramatic beauty. Fjords were pushed up millions of years ago by gigantic glaciated ice, and their valleys have been carved into a labyrinth of waterways for people to discover and explore their nooks and crannies.

In Kenai Fjords National Park, paddle a few miles into the fjords where they reach deep into the coastline above the treeline, surrounded by dark green forest and hanging cliffs, where you're more likely to see marine wildlife up close: seals, porpoises darting under your kayak, or a whale breaching in the distance. It's amazingly quiet, the quiet sound of paddling, the sounds of nature, nothing more.

Options for kayaking tours offer something for everyone, no matter how expert you are. Half-day excursions are a great way to get a taste of the fjords. These shorter trips are perfect for someone who wants a gentle experience without having to commit to a full day on the water.

Trips like Sunny Cove Kayaking's are also perfect for beginners or those who are short on time. Full-day or multi-day tours allow you to get further into the fjord's beauty and see more of what the landscape has to offer, perhaps camping overnight. These tours are offered by small-group companies such as Liquid Adventures to ensure your experience is as personal as possible.

Group tours are a good way for you to meet new friends, share the experience together, and private tours are flexible for you to design a trip to your own interests. Whether you wish to experience a new group of people or enjoy a trip with your own small group, it's up to you. What do you want to get from this experience? Choose a tour that can provide you with what you are looking for.

One of the most popular kayaking destinations is Kenai Fjords National Park on the Kenai Peninsula, where glaciers dominate the view and marine life abounds beneath the surface. While kayaking on the open waters, kayakers have an unobstructed view of the glaciers and can witness firsthand the rush of ice and cascading waters that have carved out these majestic landscapes.

Alaska is also a prime spot for kayaking in sheltered water protected from wind and waves. One such area that is perfect for kayaking beginners is Prince William Sound. The calm waters of this fjord are home to a wealth of wildlife and dramatic scenery. As an example of the spellbinding effect of Alaska, kayaking in this area brings paddlers into an intimacy with nature, where the spirit of Alaska is revealed in each passing moment.

Kayaking Checklist

- **Tour Selection:** Choose half-day, full-day, group, or private tours.
- **Essential Gear:** Dry suit, life jacket, paddle, and weather-appropriate clothing.

- **Safety Tips:** Check the weather forecast, make sure your gear is serviceable, and know your limits.

Kayaking Alaska's fjords, you can unplug from the modern world and plug into the wild one: to see Alaska, to experience it, to paddle through a paleontological and morphological wonderland, to bear witness, on a boat, to the planet as it was, and as it's becoming. Frenetic and tranquil, mundane and exhilarating, the waterway has long held a kind of magic. It's another world.

Glacier Trekking Adventures

Imagine putting your boots on a glacier, hearing them crackle, creak, and crunch with every step, and feeling as if you couldn't be further from the hustle and bustle of daily life. Trekking on a glacier in Alaska is unlike anything you could experience in ordinary life.

The mesmerizing, surreal beauty of the landscape is bottomless and timeless. Nothing feels more alien than the barren, frozen environment of a glacier, yet nothing can make you feel, at the same time, more at home than the exhilarating, awe-inspiring experience of being on a glacier. On a glacier, you are greeted by a landscape that, on a bright sunny day, is bathed in light that reflects and refracts in ways as yet unknown to human scientific inquiry.

You could spend a lifetime exploring the blue crevassed mazes of the glacier and not be able to predict the shifting patterns of light. This is truly a landscape where time has slowed down. The ice around your feet might have been formed thousands of years ago, yet it is still alive and constantly changing. You could step through a crevasse one day and not be able to do so the next day.

This is the transient nature of the glacier; its beauty lies not only in its ever-changing nature but also in its ever-present timelessness. You could take thousands of photographs—every single one would be unique; every one would be a vision of exquisite beauty. The seemingly chaotic patterns of crevasses and ridges are created by nature's slow, steady hand, carving a dynamic environment of stunning beauty. Even when you think you've seen it all, you've only scratched the surface.

The blue maze of crevasses becomes a tunnel of light when you step inside an ice cave. What was an enticing glow when viewed from outside transforms once you enter the cave; the walls sparkle like a cathedral of ice-lit light. You can almost hear the buzzing sounds of pollinating insects, even though the cave is completely silent. The size and beauty of the views from the glacier are nearly limitless, stretching out in all directions, and everything you see is utterly captivating.

To enjoy glacier trekking, you need to prepare physically and mentally. Whether you are with an instructor or heading into the glacier alone, the trek is all about physical endurance and technical know-how. Basic ice climbing techniques, like how to use crampons and an ice axe, are invaluable skills.

A decent level of fitness is a huge advantage, and you need to muster up all your physical endurance to tackle a glacier. Uneven terrain and tricky crevasses make navigating the glacier anything but straightforward. It's important to take a realistic view of your fitness, as it is definitely possible to get yourself into a situation you cannot easily get out of if you aren't careful.

In addition to providing the safety of experience, a good guide adds to your experience on the glacier. These are not just hikes; they're educational tours. With a good guide, you'll learn the glacier's history, ecology, and geology. There are companies that offer guided educational tours, and those are especially good opportunities to visit a glacier. There is so much to learn there, from the processes that formed the glacier to the forces that shape our planet. Not only that, but a guide knows the glacier. It's their job to know the nuances that make certain paths safe and others dangerous, which parts are interesting, and which are not.

A guide turns the trek into an adventure. They're the only ones who know all the answers, which makes it possible for you to enjoy the experience fully—to focus on the adventure in front of you and the people around you, where the guide handles the logistics and safety.

Alaska is home to many iconic glaciers that are well-suited to trekking. The Matanuska Glacier is easily accessible from Anchorage, and it's a great option for beginners, offering terrain suitable for people of all ability levels, from gentle slopes to airy crevasses and ice caves.

The Matanuska is a playground. The Root Glacier in Wrangell-St. Elias National Park is deep in the wilderness and offers a more rugged experience. The terrain is rougher, and even on your way to the ice, you feel as though you've entered a wilderness untouched by people. Glaciers are all a bit different, and each offers its own insights into the natural world and ice.

Glacier travel is an adventure into another world, where the only logic is the logic of ice. The terrain is alien, full of surprises, and often hard work. Yet there are moments of contemplation, even wonder. What you're doing is nothing less than becoming a part of a story—a story that has been unfolding for millennia.

The Thrill of Dog Sledding

Dog sledding in Alaska is history in motion, putting you in touch with the pioneer spirit of the state. Feel the wind in your face and the rhythmic panting of huskies in the crisp air as you stand on the back of a sled and are pulled through a snowy wilderness of towering spruce and pine trees.

You will feel the adrenaline rush as you experience the true romance of Alaskan dog sledding. This iconic experience is very much tied to the legendary race of the Iditarod—the official dog sled race that follows the historic mail route from Anchorage to Nome. But the Iditarod is more than just a race. It is a re-enactment of an Alaska fur trader town's pioneering past, when mushers and their dogs delivered mail over hundreds of frozen miles.

Bonding with the sled dogs is also part of the delight. Dogs are dogs, and these dogs are athletes, bred for endurance and strength, yet they're also playful. They're not unresponsive beasts. If you spend time with them before the ride, you get to know them individually, their quirks, the way they relate to their mushers, and you can feel that connection as they pull the sled, each with his or her own role, bound together by their team spirit and the musher's calls. This dance of motion and companionship is very humbling, but also exhilarating.

If you're thinking about going dog sledding, it helps to know what to expect. During the course of a typical itinerary, you'll learn about the history of mushing, the handling of a healthy, happy team, and how they are cared for.

You will pull a sled through a blurry white and green world, hearing only the crunch of snow and the occasional husky's bark. You'll listen to the mushers tell stories of the trail and mushing tips. You'll gain a deeper understanding of the skill and effort it takes to handle a team through the wild.

The sled riding experience changes depending on the season and location. In winter, the sled skims over snow, allowing for a more traditional mushing experience. In summer, however, the sleds typically have wheels affixed, allowing for a dry land experience.

This experience mimics the winter tradition, just on land, and allows for the possibility of mushing without the bite of winter. On snow or wheels, the ride is always a one-of-a-kind experience in getting to see Alaska through the eyes of a sled dog.

It's also crucial to consider ethical concerns when you choose a dog sledding operator. Look for companies that proudly keep their dogs in good health and treat them with respect.

Seek out operators who meet high standards for sled dog care—dogs that are provided with adequate rest, are fed a nutritious diet, and receive regular veterinary care.

Ask questions: how do they train their dogs? What do their dogs do in the off-season? How do they keep their dogs healthy and happy? A responsible operator will welcome these questions and will be happy to tell you about the steps they take to provide good care for their dogs.

Dog sledding in Alaska is an experience unlike any other. It's an education in state history, an opportunity to share in the living legacy of an exceptionally intimate relationship between humans and dogs. It's not just about riding in a sled; it's about being a part of a way of life that has formed the Alaskan spirit for centuries—a moment unto itself, when history, nature, and adventure conspire in a singular experience.

Ziplining Over Alaskan Landscapes

Picture yourself flinging yourself from a launch platform several stories above the ground, harness cinched tight around your waist, hair flying as you hurtle through the air, wind howling in your ears, the wilderness of Alaska whizzing by below as you zip from perch to perch—an array of verdant forests and rocky peaks, sun-glinting rivers, and mountain passes—landscapes that, for birds, would be seen in flight.

Zipping through the air is a heady mix—the sensation of flight and panoramas seen from the air, all in one destination. In an instant you're in flight, clipping from one point to the next, blurring through the air, your heart pounding to the rhythm of the wind. A heart-pounding adrenaline rush, ziplining is a rush for anyone who enjoys the thrill of a fast ride, a dizzying plunge, a thrill-ride experience, and an adventure that won't soon be forgotten as you take in Alaska from on high.

Do your research before heading out—this is your opportunity for exploration and adventure, and zipline courses vary greatly in length and height. Think about what kind of experience you're looking for; some ziplines are more than a mile long, allowing you to take in the view at a leisurely pace, while others are much shorter, guaranteeing a quick fix of adrenaline.

Depending on where your adventure takes place, your experience could also be vastly different. The ZipRider at Icy Strait Point in Hoonah (northwest of Juneau) is one of the world's longest and steepest ziplines and can reach speeds of up to 60 miles per hour.

As you zip by at warp speed over verdant forests and shimmering waters below, the view can only amplify the thrill. Or you can try Seward's Tree Top Adventure, which has shorter, slower ziplines that wind through the canopy and offer an up-close look at Alaska's abundant biodiversity.

When you're careening through the air on a zipline, it's good to know that your experience is as safe as it can be. The safety measures taken on ziplines are seen, heard, and felt throughout your entire experience.

The first thing you'll encounter before you even get on the platform is a briefing given by seasoned instructors who will walk you through the protocols. This includes having all of your straps properly and snugly, but not too tight, so that you will be comfortable and unhindered in your ability to move around.

You will also be instructed to wear your helmet, which will not only keep you safe but will also give you confidence as you get ready to launch. These briefings will also cover the basics of zipline etiquette, such as the rules of the road. For example, you will learn how to slow yourself down and how to signal to the guide if you need assistance.

Alaska is something of a mecca for zipline enthusiasts, with destinations up and down the Inside Passage offering different flavors of exhilaration and eye-popping scenery. The fastest descent in the world is at Icy Strait Point's ZipRider, where you fly toward the sea in a small pod suspended from a massive cable.

At speeds up to 60 miles per hour, you'll fly 1,300 feet above the landscape, enjoying views most people never see below. At Seward's Tree Top Adventure, you'll fly through the canopy of hemlock and spruce at slow to moderate speeds, presenting a less-thrilling, more intimate experience, where you can look down amid the trees and get a closer look at the forest ecosystem as you fly from tree to tree.

Final Thoughts

Ziplining in Alaska is not only an adrenaline-filled experience but also a unique opportunity to communicate with nature. Ziplining gives you an unusual perspective on the world. You fly over landscapes that are considered some of the most beautiful spots on Earth, but at the same time, you are a part of it.

You feel the thrill of flying, but at the same time, the way you experience Alaska is extremely satisfying. So if you are an adrenaline junkie or if you just want to try an adventure sport, ziplining is a great opportunity that you should definitely take into account.

Adapting Alaska's High-Adrenaline Adventures for Accessibility

Alaska's outdoor adventures offer exhilarating experiences for all travelers, and many tour operators provide options that make these activities more accessible to individuals with mobility or sensory needs.

For those interested in kayaking, some tour operators offer stable tandem kayaks and adaptive paddling equipment, making it easier for individuals with limited mobility or upper body strength to participate. Prince William Sound is a great choice for beginners or those who prefer calmer waters, and some guided tours launch from accessible docks to accommodate travelers with physical limitations.

For glacier trekking, Matanuska Glacier is one of the most accessible options, as it is reachable by road and offers guided hikes for varying skill levels. Travelers who may not be able to navigate the ice on foot can still enjoy spectacular glacier views from observation points or boat tours near major tidewater glaciers like Hubbard Glacier or Exit Glacier.

Dog sledding tours can also be adapted to different needs. While traditional mushing requires standing and balancing on a sled, many operators provide seated sled options, allowing participants to experience the thrill of the ride without needing to stand. For those who prefer a dry-land experience, summer dog cart rides offer an alternative that allows visitors to meet the dogs and enjoy a gentler ride on wheels rather than snow.

Ziplining can be challenging for travelers with limited mobility or balance concerns, but some courses, such as Seward's Tree Top Adventure, offer lower-speed, controlled experiences. Travelers should consult with operators in advance to discuss harness requirements, accessibility options, and safety measures.

For those who may not be able to physically participate in these activities, Alaska still offers breathtaking ways to experience its landscapes, such as boat-based glacier and wildlife tours, flightseeing over fjords, and accessible scenic viewpoints. By selecting the right tour and planning ahead, everyone can find a way to connect with Alaska's stunning wilderness in a way that suits their abilities and comfort levels.

Chapter Eight

The Inside Passage Experience

The Inside Passage, a 1,500-mile-long route through the northernmost reaches of North America, is a waterway that winds through some of Alaska's most beautiful destinations.

Your vessel cruises past islands and inlets, around sharp bends, and around seemingly endless corners. It's an undeniably lovely stretch of water. The Inside Passage is also one of the most dynamic arteries of travel in The Last Frontier, a place that connects physically remote communities, and a protected route that permits ships to avoid the destructive fury of the Pacific during the region's fierce winter storms. More than two million cruise passengers travel through the waterway each year.

This means that, especially for those who chart this waterway, it is no easy passage. Tides make rapids out of places where they are normally deep, and timing those rapids requires fine control of schedules and knowledge of slack water (the window of time between high and low tides when currents are at their lowest) to move safely from point A to point B.

In addition to the intricacies of where to find slack water, mariners must also be aware of the exact time information in detailed current tables and local knowledge. Pilots—experienced mariners familiar with the passage—provide guidance to larger vessels for a fee, going aboard to share knowledge gleaned from years of experience.

If you choose your vessel wisely, it will determine your entire Inside Passage experience. Those who opt for a small vessel will experience a much more intimate adventure, often accessing ports well out of reach for most larger ships. On a small ship, you'll get a cozy, casual experience that's focused on what Alaska has to offer in the way of natural wonders, without having to deal with a large crowd of fellow passengers trying to do the same thing.

Opt for a big ship, and you get a floating resort experience, with more onboard activities and entertainment than you'll ever have time to try. Entertainment options include shows in the ships' theaters, visits to the spa, and a wide range of dining venues.

Today, the Inside Passage is navigated with greater safety and efficiency than ever before. Modern GPS and radar systems provide captains and crews with real-time data on the ship's position and the surrounding environment. This allows crews to anticipate changing tides and weather patterns, adjusting their course accordingly.

Real-time weather data is also critical, as conditions in the Inside Passage can change rapidly. With access to live weather forecasts, crews can be better prepared for their journey by adapting to changing conditions that could easily disrupt their planned course. With the right tools, the Inside Passage turns from an arduous boating route into a well-mapped pathway.

Whether you cruise through the passage on a small ship or aboard a larger vessel, you will be in a world where nature and travel come together. The Inside Passage is a place of history and scenery, of culture and community, of discovery and anticipation. The journey is far more than a route; it is an experience, an opportunity to delve deeper into the beauty and complexity of Alaska.

Hidden Gems Along the Inside Passage

One is Petersburg, sometimes called 'Little Norway,', worth a visit if you are up for getting off the ship and exploring a bit. It is one of those beautiful seaside Alaskan towns with Norwegian settlers that began arriving in the late 19th century, giving this part of Alaska its unique Norwegian-Alaskan flavor. The streets with their colorful wooden houses reflect Scandinavian heritage. This is a water-oriented community with fishing being at the core of the town. Its annual Little Norway Festival celebrates this heritage with traditional dances, music, and lots of local seafood.

There is also the Anan Wildlife Observatory, perhaps one of the very best places in the US to observe bears in the wild. Also part of the Tongass, it is open between May and September. In the summer, bears fish for salmon in the river below, and there is an excellent viewing platform where you can watch them.

Bald eagles and seals also gather at the site. It is as close as you can get to wilderness and yet be able to spend time watching bears go about their business. Standing quietly on the deck, in the company of others who share your sense of wonder, is humbling and often exhilarating.

While these sites are undeniably beautiful, they are also important cultural and ecological hotspots: in Petersburg, there are local art and craft markets where the artisans sell what they make (from intricate carvings and knives to handmade jewelry and clothing) and are often willing to chat with visitors about their traditions.

Anan is a global biodiversity hotspot: the forest and waterways are teeming with plant and animal life. The ecosystems are fragile and complicated, and the variety of life is stunning.

Sometimes getting to these out-of-the-way spots is half the adventure. Smaller cruise lines often have these destinations on their itinerary. Or you could splurge on a local charter so that you can go at your own pace. Public ferries will also get you to a lot of these spots, and the ride there is half the fun (and very cost-effective). The Alaska Marine Highway System provides service to many of these places, and you'll get to enjoy the scenery along the way.

Local lore helps to bring places alive too. In Petersburg, you will hear stories about those who founded the town, or about how the inhabitants had to cope in winter months with no light at all. Your guides in Anan will often also tell stories about the bears they've come to know, their quirks and habits, bringing a personality to the places you are visiting.

Insider Tips for Avoiding Tourist Traps

The Inside Passage is, of course, beautiful, but it's very easy to get stuck in a rut—going to all the places that everyone else goes. Port areas tend to resemble theme parks masquerading as Alaskan towns. Ketchikan can be overwhelmed by the crowds, and while it has many charms, you may find yourself caught up in the rush to explore famous spots like Creek Street. Some excursions promise much but deliver little more than a crowded bus ride to hurriedly jostle you into a photo opportunity, all for a premium price tag. The result is an experience that feels more like being a cog in a tourist machine than an explorer of the wild.

If you really want to experience the Inside Passage like a local, you've got to think like one. For one, take advantage of a classic Alaska strategy: show up early or later in the day. Early morning and late afternoon are typically the periods when the crowds are the thinnest and the atmosphere the quietest. It's not difficult to recognize the difference. You can wander through the dockside buildings in Ketchikan and collect your souvenirs without feeling like a strolling sardine. Or greet the morning by watching whales up close and personal.

Another way to access the authentic side of Alaska is to let the locals show you around. Local guides live here and understand the state. They can offer a perspective and passion you won't get from your brief encounter on a pre-packaged excursion. If you're lucky, you might end up with a guide who is genuinely interested in your experience and who will tell you all about the history of a tiny fishing village or show you the best views free of prickly crowds. It might not sound like much, but it can make the difference between checking off a destination on a list and making a lasting memory.

The best of the Inside Passage, though, lies just beyond the shoreline. The big port towns are filled to bursting with visitors, and while you're likely to find something enjoyable, the true gems—fresh food, local patrons, and the "real" Alaska—lie in the side streets, tucked away in back alleys, or just outside of town.

Local eateries and hidden cafés exist in every town, serving authentic Alaskan fare that isn't buried on the back pages of a tourist menu or hidden in an expensive restaurant on the main street. You might stumble across a small, family-run café in a hole-in-the-wall serving the best clam chowder you've ever had or a bakery selling berry pies that taste like sunshine and rain.

Beyond food is nature: nature trails off the main roads lead to the interior of forests, where you can move at your own pace, away from the trampling tourist hordes. From these paths, you might stumble across a vista overlooking a river or a secret cove, where you can watch wildlife undisturbed.

Arriving with your homework done makes all the difference. Doing your research well can help you avoid the tourist traps and uncover what's really worth seeing. Travel forums and reviews can be brilliant: finding firsthand accounts and tips from people who have been there before you can be invaluable. Read the most recent posts to get the latest information—things can change from season to season. Travel blogs and insider guides can make you aware of places you would otherwise have missed, and they can show you how to experience the "classic" sights in a deeper, more personal way.

They can also help you find activities to suit your interests if the main tourist offerings don't match what you want to do. Perhaps you'd prefer a quiet hike in silence rather than a noisy group outing? A visit to an artist's gallery instead of the day-tripping ferry? An afternoon in a quiet garden instead of an overcrowded concert?

It's possible, with some effort and a bit of research, to create an Inside Passage experience that is more than a well-worn checklist of stops along the water's edge.

Once you step off the beaten path, you open up opportunities to have those moments of connection that are the essence of what makes travel unforgettable.

Whether it's eating clam chowder in a local diner, admiring the view from a remote wind-swept bluff miles away from the highway, or visiting a small town's public beach, these moments will stay with you long after you return home from Alaska. Adventures, stories, and memories await those who travel with their eyes open and their minds curious.

The Best Shore Excursions

While the Inside Passage is a scenic adventure in itself, many of the shore excursions are equally tempting. In Juneau, you'll have the opportunity to go whale-watching and—with luck on your side—see a humpback whale leap out of the water and land with a splash so loud you can hear it over the engines of the touring boats.

You won't soon forget this spectacle of power and grace. A knowledgeable naturalist accompanying you on the cruise will enrich the experience with insights into the marine life and ecosystem of the area. The tour will also take you to the best viewing spots, which often are open only to these tours.

Another option is to glacier-hike out of Skagway. Here, you put on crampons and step out onto a vast expanse of ice surrounded by towering peaks and deep blue crevasses. A local guide takes you across the surface of the glacier, teaching you how it formed and how forces continue to shape it.

These guides are more than just a line of defense: they're a window into the glacier's geologic history, pulling back the veils of time to reveal a world of stories, creatures, and natural events hidden beneath your feet. The adventure allows access to areas generally off-limits to the public. And it's not expensive.

These in-demand tours do have to be booked in advance. Whale-watching and glacier-trekking are two of the most popular excursions and sell out fast. So, if you know you will be in Alaska and are excited about one of these popular activities, book as early as possible.

When you finally book your cruise, you should also check to see which shore excursions are available at each stop so that you can book those at the same time. Finally, be sure to check the schedule for your ship since there is often a limited window of time for the excursions, and you might want to get off the boat to take an excursion and still have time to enjoy the amenities on board your ship.

Safety and accessibility are two important considerations when you're booking your excursions. Prior to departure on an excursion, you'll generally receive a safety briefing, outlining everything from how to use the equipment to potential hazards to keep in mind. These are important briefings and will generally include a Q&A segment so that you can ask questions about the excursion itself.

If you're unsure, just ask. Equipment is almost always provided; if you're heading out for whale watching, you'll be given a life jacket, and if you're trekking on a glacier, crampons will be waiting for you. Many excursions are accessible, so you shouldn't have any trouble finding an excursion that works for your needs—if you are worried, just inquire.

Final Thoughts

From watching a humpback breach the cold waters of Juneau to an adventure across a glacier in Skagway, these shore excursions allow you to connect with Alaska in a way few adventures ever will. They invite you to explore and experience the natural world, to be inspired, to learn, and to live. To experience and to remember.

Exploring the Inside Passage with Accessibility in Mind

The Inside Passage offers stunning scenery, fascinating cultural sites, and incredible wildlife encounters, many of which are accessible to travelers of all abilities. For scenic cruising, modern ships are equipped with accessible decks, elevators, and seating areas, making it easy to enjoy the breathtaking views from the comfort of your ship. If you prefer a smaller vessel for a more intimate experience, be sure to check accessibility options before booking, as not all smaller ships are wheelchair-friendly.

Many Alaskan port towns, such as Petersburg and Ketchikan, have accessible boardwalks, museums, and cultural centers, allowing visitors to explore at their own pace. However, some remote wildlife-viewing locations—like Anan Wildlife Observatory—may have uneven terrain or require long walks. If mobility is a concern, look for boat-based wildlife tours or accessible boardwalks at places like Mendenhall Glacier or Sitka National Historical Park.

Whale-watching tours in Juneau are among the most accessible excursions, with most operators offering wheelchair-accessible boats with ramps and accessible seating. However, glacier hiking in Skagway and other locations can be challenging due to uneven terrain and the need for special equipment (crampons, ice axes, etc.). Travelers who prefer a less physically demanding experience can still enjoy stunning glacier views via boat tours, helicopter flights, or scenic overlooks.

For those looking to avoid the crowds and experience Alaska more authentically, choosing local-led excursions, visiting hidden cafés, or taking accessible nature trails near port towns can be a rewarding alternative to mass-market tourist attractions. By planning ahead and selecting the right tours and activities, travelers of all abilities can fully enjoy the wonders of the Inside Passage.

Chapter Nine

Voices from the Voyage

Your Feedback Makes Waves!

Thank you for embarking on this journey through Alaska with me. From the stunning glaciers to the awe-inspiring wildlife, I hope this guide has helped you plan the adventure of a lifetime.

If you found this guide useful, inspiring, or simply fun to read, I'd be thrilled to hear your thoughts! Your review not only helps me grow but also helps future adventurers find the tools they need to make their Alaskan dreams come true.

How to Leave a Review

Alaska

1. **Scan the QR code.**

2. **Fill in your review:** Share your experience—what you loved, what helped, or even what you'd like to see in future guides.

3. **Hit Submit**: Knowing your review will help me and countless others explore Alaska!

Thank you for helping me inspire travelers everywhere. Together, we're creating unforgettable journeys!

Bon Voyage,
Diana from Ocean Breeze Adventures

Chapter Ten

Immersive Experiences: From Wilderness to Wellness

You're in bed when the sun wakes you by stretching its rays up and over Tordrillo Mountain Lodge. You open your door to a blast of chilling, energizing air and listen to the sounds of majestic Alaska. You came all this way to find peace and rejuvenation in the outdoors, and the results speak for themselves. This chapter is about wellness and about finding it in Alaska's unique and unbeatable places.

Wellness Retreats

Alaska's wellness retreats are as versatile as they are wide-ranging, with adventures that combine natural landscapes and traditions with mind-body-spirit practices for nurturing well-being.

Forest Bathing in Alaska

One such retreat is a guided forest bathing experience, an ancient practice during which you are invited to immerse yourself in the sights, sounds, and smells of the forest on a walk through the trees by a facilitator trained in locating animals, plants, and the essence of the landscape. Using all your senses, you will slowly explore the surroundings and spend some time on the ground—being a part of the forest, allowing it to wash over you with the simple objective of reducing stress, relaxing your mind, and releasing old tensions. The forest becomes a sanctuary, a place to turn off your smartphone and reconnect with yourself.

Yoga Retreats

For those who prefer a little more structure, yoga retreats combine movement and stillness in sublime settings. You might rise early for a sunrise session on a mountaintop, the vista expanding your outlook as your body expands through each pose. The landscape becomes your silent accomplice, supporting your breath and heartbeat. These retreats often include mindfulness and meditation practices, helping you reflect on your physical and emotional state.

Spa Experiences

Perhaps the best way to reinvigorate the spirit is to spend an entire day or weekend in an Alaskan spa. Most spas source ingredients locally, such as mud rich in essential minerals and Alaskan seaweed, a natural detoxifier. A mud wrap draws out impurities from the skin, leaving it soft and supple, while a seaweed facial nourishes the skin with essential nutrients.

These treatments are not just indulgences; they work to improve your state of mind and encourage reconnecting with nature. By using traditional techniques developed over generations, an Alaskan spa offers a perfect blend of indulgence and therapeutic restoration.

Choosing the Right Wellness Package

While every itinerary looks great, it's vital to pick a wellness package that's right for you. Think about your reasons for going on a retreat and how you'd like to feel when you return. Detox programs typically include a combination of treatments, exercise, and nutrition that cleanse your body and mind. Rejuvenation packages often feature relaxation and stress-relief activities such as massage and aromatherapy. These itineraries may also include mindfulness sessions to help you take away tools you can use in your everyday life.

Find Your Wellness Focus

Take a moment to consider what you want from your wellness experience. What's your state of mind and body right now? What are your areas of tension or imbalance? What kind of environment will create a space for you to relax and heal? Write down your thoughts, including any specific goals or desires. This kind of exercise can help to clarify your intentions and guide your selection of where to go for your retreat or which package to choose from the spa menu.

The Alaska wilderness is "part of the experience of wellness," writes Candice Gaukel Andrews in *The Wild Within* (2008). Nature in Alaska also provides solitude and silence, but it's also tinged with awe and wonder.

Hiking Trails for All Levels

There's a trail for you, no matter your fitness or adventurousness.

Why not start with the Tony Knowles Coastal Trail in Anchorage, a welcoming introduction to the wilds of Alaska? This easy, multi-use path runs 19.7 miles but can be broken into chunks of varying lengths. Stunning views of Cook Inlet unfurl as you walk, and on the way you can see moose, eagles, and all manner of waterfowl—as well as beluga whales out in the bay. The trail is flat, open to all, and the coastal breeze creates a refreshing cool.

For those who want to test themselves a little more, the moderate Harding Icefield Trail in Kenai Fjords National Park delivers a serious reward after an 8.2-mile round-trip hike through lush forest and alpine meadow. Look out for marmots and mountain goats scurrying over the rocky crags, and expect some steep sections along the route—sturdy boots and trekking poles will help. The reward is a view over the icefield, where the sparkling blue ice stretches to the horizon.

One of the more adventurous trails, the Crow Pass Trail in Chugach State Park, is a 21-mile trek that cuts across all kinds of terrain between miles and miles of lush forest and exposed tundra and eventually, sweeping views of glaciers. It can be quite difficult, with lots of ups and downs and even with a few potential river crossings, but it is worthwhile for those who are up to the challenge and want to spend a whole day (and possibly night) in the wilderness. This trail is a spectacular place to see some wildlife, including bears and moose that are often spotted along the trail, so carry bear spray and make noise while walking.

Bring food and water with you. If it is a long hike, make sure you have enough water and something to eat that will give you energy. Dress in layers and have a rain jacket handy, even if it is sunny out. If it is a long hike, have a map and compass or a GPS with you. Tell someone where you are going and when you expect to be back.

To ensure the preservation of these natural wonders for future generations, you should also be a thoughtful hiker. Stay on marked paths to avoid damage to delicate ecosystems and pack out all your refuse, even biodegradable waste such as fruit peels that can disrupt natural wildlife diets.

Every one of these trails has its own mix—some easier, some harder, some with grand mountain views, others with views of the sea. Some start in towns or villages, others in wilderness areas. Some last for days, others only hours. Each is an opportunity to explore the raw and beautiful heart of Alaska.

Relaxing in Alaskan Hot Springs

Picture yourself in a natural hot spring, the steam floating gently above the water and a cool mountain breeze tingling your skin. These geothermal pools are often found in some of the quietest places on Earth, and besides the warmth they provide, there is an underlying sense of peace and calm.

You can lie back and gaze out at the surrounding wilderness, where the only audible sounds are leaves rustling in the wind and a bird calling in the distance. The hot water, rich in minerals, relaxes sore muscles and melts away stress so that you emerge feeling refreshed and energized.

Most people have heard of Chena Hot Springs near Fairbanks, the best-known hot springs in Alaska. They, along with a large lodge, an ice museum, and a restaurant, are part of a resort and an ideal place for a day trip or an overnight visit. Go during the cold months, when the contrasts between the warm water and the chilly air only add to the experience. Perhaps less known, but no less enjoyable, is Manley Hot Springs in Interior Alaska, where you can visit a more remote spring and get a taste of the area's private greenhouse pool with lush surroundings.

The health benefits of "taking the waters" are well known, with many visitors keen to relax and enjoy their soak, while others come to unwind and be healed. The mineral content of the water is said to be good for cleansing the skin and body, and regular soaks can improve circulation, increasing the flow of blood, and helping to reduce muscular and joint pain and inflammation.

Arthritic sufferers and those with joint conditions often report profound relief, aided by the warmth of the water, which penetrates into the muscles, providing a natural and painless form of relief. The mental health benefits, however, are just as great. People often report reduced stress and anxiety as the result of slowing down, putting everyday worries to one side, and allowing the mind to rest.

If you do visit these places, please remember to be considerate and follow the etiquette at hand—and please follow safety guidelines. If you're in a communal place, don't gawk at anyone. Speak softly. Others might be there to relax, and you don't want to disrupt them.

Make sure you stay hydrated. The heat can be dehydrating, so you should drink plenty of water before and after your soak. Don't forget to listen to your body. If you're there with others, remind each other to take cooling breaks; these, too, are a shared ritual. The combination of the elements, the landscapes, and the lush vegetation with the hot water that relaxes the body is what makes an Alaskan hot spring so special.

Photography Tours and Workshops

If you're like many people, on an Alaskan cruise you'll find yourself taking the photos of a lifetime as you explore Alaska's sprawling landscapes, from Kenai Fjords to Denali National Park. Photography tours do exactly that, offering opportunities to capture the state's spectacular scenery and improve your photography skills. As the guides drive you from place to place, they show you how to take pictures that capture the essence of Alaska while you learn technical details to help you improve your photos.

You can also get some instruction on composition and other techniques to help you make the most of your photography. These tours are for both the novice photographer and the more seasoned enthusiast wanting to refine their skills. Whatever your level of skill, you'll learn from experts who not only know the best spots to capture that perfect image but can share their insights to help you take better pictures.

Photography workshops in Alaska are as diverse as the state itself. If you're captivated by the drama created in the sky by the swirling colors of the Aurora Borealis, a night photography workshop will teach you to capture the Northern Lights at their best.

You'll learn to use long exposure settings, the advantages of a steady tripod, and how to use manual focus to create sharp images. For the person who is fascinated by the micro world, a macro photography workshop in a botanical garden will open up a new world of miniature patterns and textures that you never see. Here you'll discover the small structures of plants and insects. Each workshop teaches people how to focus on a specific interest and learn more about the aspects that appeal to them.

For those brand new to photography, basic lessons in camera settings and photographic techniques will be a must. For those with more experience, masterclasses that challenge you and encourage you to push the boundaries of your creativity in the beautiful and ever-changing landscape are a great option.

You'll also want to bear in mind that, especially in the Arctic, the margin of time between the lightest and darkest part of the day is really small, and it's essential that you're out there when the sun is rising or setting over the beautiful mountains and glaciers of Alaska, when dramatic golden light bathes the landscape. The key is having the flexibility to get there so you're not only learning in the right conditions but also practicing in the conditions you came all the way there for.

Final Thoughts

The experience of these tours and workshops is often revelatory, as attested by participants who have found new confidence and appreciation of the world through their lens. For the photographer, Alaska provides a seemingly endless opportunity to see and capture nature's beauty. Whether you take an Alaska photography tour or workshop, you can enhance your skills, capture memories, and really connect with nature in a way that is creative, rewarding, and fun.

As you pull up the camera to your eye and hear the click of the shutter, you are inviting yourself to see the world in a brand new way. When the camera comes down, you'll take away memories that last a lifetime. As you continue on your journey throughout Alaska, bring your camera and take home the wildness of a place where nature's beauty and the art of photography meet.

Finding Wellness & Relaxation in Alaska with Accessibility in Mind

Alaska's vast and peaceful landscapes offer a wide range of wellness experiences that cater to travelers of all abilities. Forest bathing, yoga retreats, and spa experiences are often held in locations with accessible trails, ramps, or flexible accommodations to ensure that all participants can fully enjoy their restorative benefits.

For hiking enthusiasts, Alaska offers both challenging backcountry trails and accessible nature paths. The Tony Knowles Coastal Trail in Anchorage is one of the best options for wheelchair users and those who prefer level, paved paths, while more advanced hikers can explore Harding Icefield Trail or Crow Pass Trail. If hiking on foot is not an option, many scenic overlooks and boat tours offer breathtaking views of glaciers, mountains, and wildlife.

Hot springs provide a deeply relaxing experience, and Chena Hot Springs near Fairbanks is one of the most accessible options. The resort features paved walkways, accessible changing areas, and hot springs pools that can accommodate most mobility needs. Visitors should check in advance for any additional accessibility considerations at more remote hot springs like Manley Hot Springs, which may require additional steps or uneven terrain.

For those looking to capture the beauty of Alaska through photography, many tours and workshops offer accessible alternatives. Wildlife and Northern Lights photography can often be done from accessible viewing platforms, boats, or designated scenic overlooks without requiring long treks into the wilderness. Visitors should inquire ahead of time about transportation options and accessible facilities to ensure a comfortable and enjoyable experience.

With careful planning, Alaska's wellness and relaxation experiences can be fully enjoyed by travelers seeking rejuvenation, no matter their level of mobility or physical ability. Whether it's soaking in a steamy natural hot spring, meditating in a serene forest, or capturing the magic of the Northern Lights through a camera lens, there's an accessible path to finding peace and inspiration in the Last Frontier.

Chapter Eleven

Culinary Delights of Alaska

It's hard to imagine a more fitting introduction to Alaskan cuisine than a hearty breakfast in a cozy diner, the smell of reindeer sausage sizzling on the grill blending with the aroma of freshly brewed coffee. But this breakfast is only the beginning of the journey, a path that leads far beyond the plate and into the state's cultural heart.

To really understand what Alaska is all about, you have to understand its food—not just the dishes on your plate, but the interwoven tapestry of the land, the people, and the history that has made this place what it is. From the icy waters where the sweetest King Crab is born to the wild berries that dot the tundra, every ingredient has a story, a tale of survival and tradition. To experience Alaskan cuisine is to celebrate the land itself.

Must-Try Local Dishes and Where to Find Them

Alaskan cuisine is a mosaic of tastes. Reindeer sausage—a local favorite—is often served at breakfast. It's a gamey, spicy sausage with a deep, rich flavor. It's a staple for many Alaskans. Akutaq, also known as Eskimo ice cream, is a traditional dish made of wild berries and animal fat. It's creamy and sweet, and it's more about the texture than the taste. And of course, there's Alaskan King Crab—the sweet, succulent meat. Steamed, grilled, or served with butter sauce, it's all good.

You'll want to seek out these pleasures in places that feel authentic, where preparation and presentation capture the state's spirit. For example, in Anchorage, you'll find family-run restaurants with intimate atmospheres, serving up reindeer sausage prepared with love and care, cooked in the traditional way.

These restaurants pride themselves on using ingredients sourced locally as much as possible, so you know that you are eating true Alaskan grub when you eat here. Along the coast, seafood shacks serve King Crab straight from the ocean, often with a great view of the water.

It is a casual atmosphere that allows you to eat and enjoy your food without the frills, putting the focus on flavor and freshness, not presentation or ambiance. Simon & Seafort's Saloon & Grill, in Anchorage, has been serving some of the best seafood around, including King Crab, for years and is a favorite of locals and visitors alike.

The story behind these dishes is as interesting as the flavors themselves. Reindeer sausage is made from the sorts of game meats that Alaska has in abundance, and an understanding of the state's reliance on its natural resources is reflected in the ways in which the sausage is made: the process has been a multi-generational transformation of a relatively simple idea of what you do with meat in large quantities, and each family has its own little trick or twist, an additional ingredient that makes theirs the best.

Akutaq also has its origins in necessity. Indigenous peoples created the dish from what was available to them to make a tasty treat that also fueled the body—ingredients such as berries, primarily blueberries and salmonberries (also known as the red huckleberry), foraged from the wild, burst with the taste of Alaska. King crab is sourced from the cold waters surrounding the state and reflects Alaska's abundance of marine life as well as its sustainably managed fisheries.

Local cooks are the custodians of all of that, and each cook brings their own passion, experience, and expertise to bear on the ingredients. Many have been cooking for years, some relying on traditional cooking and preparing methods, and others using modern techniques to create new, innovative dishes that are deeply rooted in history.

A chef might tell you about a recipe for reindeer sausage that was passed down from their grandmother or how they have learned to perfect the fat-to-berry ratio in an akutaq. There is a depth of story that comes along with this kind of food, a connection to people and place.

The Art of Alaskan Beading and Crafts

Walk into a community hall in Alaska, and you'll find a space that's buzzing with conversation and laughter and the clack-clack-clack of beads being worked on. For many Alaskans, beading and other crafts are part of their cultural identity. Beaded regalia is a prominent part of cultural celebrations here.

Brightly hued garments are embellished with symbols and patterns that are meaningful to each community. They are worn to celebrations and ceremonies and serve as a means to pass on stories from one generation to the next. Crafting is not a solitary activity here; it is communal. People gather to share techniques and stories and craft things together that represent their shared history.

The culinary experience and craft often overlap, enriching the dining experience in surprising ways. Setting the table with beaded table settings makes a meal more elegant and all the more enjoyable by infusing it with history.

Their patterns reflect the beauty of nature, like the landscape of Alaska. Crafted objects aren't just functional: they are a celebration of the artistry that defines Alaskan culture. Food festivals have craft markets set up beside food stalls, and a feast for the eyes accompanies the feast for the stomach. Artisans display their beaded jewelry, their carved utensils, and the skill and care taken in making them can be appreciated by the diners.

Beading workshops may also be part of cultural centers where visitors can participate in making their own beaded designs. For some travelers, this beading experience is their only hands-on interaction with Alaska Natives.

There are also the artisans who continue to craft and experiment in an effort to preserve and innovate, some of them mashing up old traditions with new influences and materials to produce work that is valuable to both local communities and a global audience. There's the story of an artisan who uses modern materials in their work to create pieces that attract a global audience, as well as local communities who might find the work more "authentic" than others.

Behind every piece of art, there is a story to tell: the stories of the artisan, and the audiences that come into contact with the art. They're stories of identity, resilience, and creativity.

Exploring Local Markets and Eateries

Stepping into an Alaskan market is like peeling back time. It transports you back to a world of untainted color, sweet perfumes, and warm community. In Anchorage, the Anchorage Market Festival is not just stalls; it is a visual, olfactory, and aural feast. Artisans, farmers, and food stands of all stripes converge to share Alaska's finest wares.

Dances whip through the aisles as locals and tourists alike shop the treasures. Scent wafts through the air: bread baking, food sautéing, dough frying. It's an energetic, fast-paced, high-volume outing. The Sitka Farmers Market, meanwhile, is quieter. Situated in scenic Harrigan Centennial Hall, it boasts local vegetables and crafts.

It's a slow-paced experience, a reserved and thoughtful take on the bounty of the Alaskan harvest. Vendors there are folksy and warm, happy to share the story of a product and the traditions behind it.

These markets can be as interesting as they are rewarding, and getting the most out of them can be enhanced by a few tips. The best time to visit is early in the day, as it is quieter, meaning you get to pick the freshest food and finest handicrafts, and there are no crowds.

Mornings can be more leisurely too: the vendors have time to chat with you and can often tell you a story about the object they are selling or recommend a local specialty. Ask for some samples—most vendors will offer you something for free to taste to help you decide. This is a great way to meet people, learn about the culture, try new things, and support the local economy.

The culinary scene, like the land itself, is vast and varied. Come to Alaska and follow the food trail through some of the state's main locations, and you'll discover off-the-beaten-path hot spots that even some locals might overlook. In small towns across Alaska, family-run diners offer comfort food and home cooking that's as warm and welcoming as the people who serve it. Hidden from the main tourist thoroughfares, some of these spots serve up flavors that are as traditional as Alaskan culture.

Be it an inviting cabin with a crackling fire or a cozy café with mountain views, each spot offers its own slice of Alaskan life served on a plate. There are also iconic historical establishments, repositories of local history that allow you to take a bite out of the past while sitting down to a meal. Menus at these diners often emphasize local ingredients and feature dishes with a nod to traditional preparation methods but with a modern twist.

Seasonal Alaskan markets offer new flavors along with the cycle of the seasons. Spring brings fiddlehead ferns, their dark green curling tips a promise of the flavors to come. Young, tender, and delicately bitey, this green is a locals' favorite, typically sautéed with garlic or served raw in salads. When the summer season comes to a close, fall markets are stocked with foraged mushrooms, each with a distinct taste and texture: the nutty chanterelle and the meaty porcini. The seasons dictate what is available, and, as the tides change, so too do the tastes of each season.

Indulging in Seafood Delicacies

In Alaska, seafood is less of an entrée and more of a way of life. The state's waters are teeming with marine bounty. It's no wonder seafood is so integral to Alaskan dining. It's so fresh, in fact, that many varieties of fish and shellfish move from sea to table in a matter of hours.

That immediacy is what makes Alaska's seafood so special, allowing flavors to shine that are unadulterated and as fresh as the day the seafood was caught. Alaska is also a leader in sustainable fishing practices, with a long-standing tradition of working to protect fish populations and ensure that these delicacies are enjoyed for generations to come. Sustainability and great taste? It's a win-win all around.

Salmon, without a doubt, is the king of the table: the glorious, soft, buttery texture of the flesh is so delicious it will shine in any dish, whether grilled, smoked, or baked. And halibut, renowned for its white, firm, flaky meat and delicate flavor, is excellent served with a squeeze of lemon and pan-fried or zestily piquant in complicated preparations.

The freshest fish is always best, so try to shop for your halibut and salmon early in the day, preferably at the fish market, where you can choose your fish from the refrigerated cases. Look for firm flesh with bright, clear eyes and a clean, oceanic aroma.

Grilling and smoking are traditional techniques that complement the natural flavors of Alaskan seafood. With salmon, a simple marinade of lemon, garlic, and dill brings out the richness of a perfect piece of fish, while a cedar plank provides a bit of smoke.

With smoked salmon, the result is an indulgent delicacy, a hearty bite that says, "This is worth savoring." It's also perfect for pairing with other bites. That's the beauty of grilling and smoking – they don't mask the flavor of the seafood, they highlight it, so there's no need for filler, distraction, or disguise. The integrity of the seafood is intact, and each bite is worthy of celebration.

Alaska's commitment to sustainable fishing is evident in the various certification programs in place to ensure that all seafood is responsibly harvested. Doing so helps to maintain fish populations and the delicate environments in which they thrive.

Choosing certified seafood helps to support practices that enable fishing to be a sustainable industry for many years to come, both for the environment and for the communities that depend on it. Fishing is a way of life in Alaska. Local fisheries are a key source of community livelihoods, providing jobs and helping to support families. When you experience Alaskan seafood, you're sharing in a tradition that supports both people and the planet.

Seafood festivals are an excellent way to dive headfirst into the Alaskan riches. The Kodiak Crab Festival celebrates all things crab—from steamed crab legs with butter to crab cakes with remoulade sauce, bacon-wrapped crab wrapped in spinach, crab fritters, and crab dips—anything crab-related.

Every year, the festival takes place in Kodiak, the nation's largest city, with a population of just under 7,000 (mostly fishermen), located about 300 miles southwest of Anchorage. Aside from the traditional festival activities of music, games, and revelry, the event celebrates sustainable seafood. The Seward Silver Salmon Derby attracts thousands of anglers who battle against each other to catch the largest (and hopefully tastiest) fish.

Final Thoughts

To experience these delicacies—whether it is slinging salmon off a grill at the Salmonfest cookoff or preparing to splay a fresh king for your own dinner table—is to participate in the long history of Alaska's culinary traditions. It's not just about taste; it's about place, about the relationship between people and the sea. Every bite of wild salmon or halibut emerging from your pan is a reflection of the work that has gone into having it on your plate.

Chapter Twelve

Environmental Stewardship and Eco-Friendly Travel

You're standing on the shore in Alaska, where the temperature is cool, and the horizon is a mix of blues and whites. Out on the sea, there is a calm and unruffled expanse of water. But that water tells a story. Invisible to the eye, the glaciers that fed this water are retreating faster than at any other time in the past hundred years, remaking the landscape in ways that are both beautiful and worrisome.

Because of these environmental changes, it's difficult to look at this scene and not see the environmental problems facing Alaska today. Natural changes to environmental conditions can be seen in the local ecosystems, but also in people's lives.

Because climate change is a force of nature, and because it is dramatic in its effects and enduring in its impact, it is real and happening now. The glaciers, once massive and seemingly infinite, are in retreat. This is the most visible sign of change. Glaciers are ancient landforms, shaped and reshaped by ice, and have spent untold millennia gouging out valleys and defining landscapes.

Today, these masses of ice are retreating in response to rising global temperatures. This melting contributes to rising sea levels, which, in turn exacerbate coastal erosion, threatening communities and the land itself. Villages located on the coast that were once secure are now threatened by the possibility of relocation as sea levels encroach on the land.

Permafrost is thawing causing once-stable ground surfaces to melt, threatening infrastructure, including roads and homes. Ecosystems are also being destabilized, affecting the complex web of life that has defined Alaska for centuries.

Ripple Effects Across Ecosystems

Climate change ripples across ecosystems, changing habitats and the species that depend upon them. Species migrate in response to these shifting habitats and in search of food, a process that is accelerating as species try to reach new habitats before their old ones become too warm. Birds and marine species change migration routes, sometimes showing up earlier or later than before, altering the food resources available to animals who are used to encountering them at a different time.

Invasive species or plants that were previously restricted to warmer climates are spreading north into Alaska, taking advantage of the warmer climate and replacing native species that can't survive in the heat. The species shuffling within ecosystems changes which animals can survive, as some species become competitors for other species and change the conditions in which they are forced to live. Many animals and plants won't survive in the rapidly changing conditions. Adaptation or extinction will be the choice.

Personal Consequences for Communities

For many of these communities, these environmental changes have profoundly personal consequences. Many Indigenous and local communities depend on the land and sea for their livelihoods, practicing subsistence hunting, fishing, and gathering as their ancestors have for generations. When sea levels rise and glaciers retreat, hunting and fishing grounds that have been passed down through the generations become inaccessible and food security is threatened.

The associated cultural practices are also under threat as the loss of land and landscapes can erode cultural heritage and identity. The cultural landscape is tied to the community's sense of identity and place and, as such, losing a piece of land is losing a piece of history.

The relocation of entire villages due to coastal erosion is another very real prospect as families are faced with the harsh choice of whether to leave the only home they know behind or face destitution. The cultural and economic impacts of these changes are huge and transformative, as people adapt the way they interact with the land.

Take a moment to think about how climate change could affect your own community and what you could do to help. How does this knowledge affect the way you think about travel and stewardship of the natural world? What can you do to promote sustainability in your own life and when you visit new places?

Eco-Friendly Travel Tips and Practices

Picture waking up in the morning in a cozy eco-lodge tucked away in the heart of Alaska. As the coffee brews, you sit by the window gazing at towering pines and snow-topped peaks. The lodges themselves are run on renewable energy sources such as solar panels, and the water is recycled, so your stay has as little impact on the environment as possible.

When you choose to stay at an eco-lodge, you support a business that looks to minimize its impact on nature and, by doing so, maintain it in its natural state. It's also an opportunity to enjoy nature and know that you're an active part of its preservation.

When it comes to getting around, try using public transport or sharing rides with other travelers. Not only are you minimizing your carbon footprint, you're being introduced to people who share your adventurous spirit. Imagine swapping stories on a bus, or meeting a hiker while sharing a car ride to a remote hiking trail. Along the way, you make new friends and are enriched by shared experiences.

As you travel, think about ways to appropriately dispose of your waste, including the often-overlooked plastic waste that can result from single-use plastics, especially in pristine environments. Carrying your own reusable water bottle and utensils is a great way to reduce plastic waste. Most communities in Alaska have water refill stations, so you can stay hydrated while minimizing your use of plastic bottles.

Take part in community recycling efforts as well. Many communities in Alaska have robust recycling programs, and sorting waste and using designated bins can help support these efforts. It's a small action with a big impact: keeping Alaska's landscapes clean and beautiful for everyone to enjoy.

When it comes to eating and shopping, conscious consumers can make a difference. Eat local, organic food whenever possible. Alaska's farmers' markets are packed with locally grown produce, locally caught seafood, and artisanal products of all kinds. When you do that, you get great ingredients, sure – but you also support local farmers and local businesses making those food choices with their eyes open to ecological and social considerations.

You're voting with your dollars to reinforce those choices, and that's a cycle that can be powerfully positive. The same is true of eco-friendly local businesses. Maybe it's a souvenir store that sources its products ethically, or a restaurant that makes a point of serving sustainably harvested seafood.

Slow travel invites you to slow down and savor the moment. It encourages you to stay longer in fewer places to allow for deeper interaction with the environment. It is here that you will truly be rewarded with the unexpected, the hidden waterfall, that special conversation with the artisan, and a greater sense of satisfaction with your journey.

Low-impact activities such as hiking, kayaking, or fishing not only lend themselves to enhanced understanding – they are a form of positive impact. Footprints, bikes, and paddles leave no trace. Hiking along a trail in Alaska or paddling through its fjords gives you an intimate sense of the landscape, a peace and tranquility with nature that is not possible from a larger vessel.

Ultimately, responsible travel is about mindful choices: honoring the places we visit, feeling pleasure in sustainable choices, and understanding that individual actions add up to global impact. And as a traveler in Alaska, you're part of a community, working to preserve a destination for posterity.

Supporting Local Conservation Efforts

A dozen or so local conservationists have gathered in a small community center. The energy is palpable. Community-led conservation projects can do a lot to help preserve some of Alaska's unique ecosystems. The state has so much beauty. Alaskans are so devoted to preserving it. Step in. Volunteer with local conservation groups. Help to restore a trail. Plant native species. Monitor wildlife. Your hands-on contribution can make a difference.

True, it's not just about the physical work. It's about making new friends. It's about giving back. It's about doing your part to preserve Alaska's wonders.

Financial donations are another valuable contribution to ensure conservation activities. Organizations such as the Alaska Conservation Foundation provide funding for projects that focus on conservation of Alaska's environment.

Your donations allow for funding of research, education, and preservation. Many conservation projects rely on the donations to conduct their operations. Projects need to purchase equipment, staff and conduct outreach programs, which all require funding. Some permits or passes fund conservation; in national parks, some of the pass money goes directly to support trails and their maintenance for future enjoyment.

Citizen science projects, some of which can be done while traveling, also allow you to combine travel with working as a researcher. These programs connect you with scientists and their work and enable you to participate in research by collecting, recording, or observing data. People of all ages and backgrounds can participate.

You don't need to be a scientist or climatologist to join wildlife monitoring programs that track the migration routes of caribou or to take part in a study that observes and measures the behavior of migrating birds. These projects allow regular people to contribute to real science and help researchers study and protect Alaska's ecosystems.

You can also participate in data collection for climate studies, which often includes measuring snowfall, recording daily temperatures, or documenting changes in plant life. As a participant, you become part of a much larger climate-monitoring effort.

Learning about conservation and environmental stewardship can be an enriching experience, and guided ecology walks and educational tours at national parks and other areas are a great way to immerse yourself in nature. These tours, led by naturalists with extensive knowledge of the local flora and fauna, will help you to learn more about the unique ecosystem present in a specific region.You will also have a better understanding of how each species plays a role in maintaining the balance of the ecosystem.

If you have an interest in environmental issues, you might also consider attending a workshop focused on sustainable living practices. During such a workshop, you can learn to distinguish between various eco-products and make the right choices when it comes to energy and waste. A workshop could cover topics such as the use of renewable energy, sustainable gardening, or waste reduction techniques.

While the Alaska Rivers, Trails & Conservation Assistance Program doesn't do trail work, it does work directly with local groups to improve trails, protect waterways, and support outdoor recreation. Through the Iditarod National Historic Trail Southern Trek, projects such as these could reconnect communities to the wild and continue to foster stewardship for the land. Getting involved in projects like these not only helps preserve a wild Alaska, it also helps bind communities closer to the land.

By volunteering, giving to local conservation organizations, participating in citizen science, or learning about Alaska's living wild places, you are literally becoming a part of Alaska's story.

Wildlife Preservation and You

Picture yourself looking across the Alaskan landscape, where the dynamic relationships among life forms maintain the health of the ecosystem as a whole. Every creature, from the smallest insect to the most powerful grizzly bear, plays some role in the ecosystem's functioning. Apex predators such as the wolf and the bear are especially important in ecosystem functioning because they regulate the populations of prey animals, which in turn affect the vegetation they consume.

By keeping populations of both predators and prey in balance, these top-rung animals help to maintain diversity in an ecosystem and its resilience to stress. Biodiversity supports a web of life that contains a broad diversity of species, each of which contributes to the ecological richness of the region. The richer the ecosystem, the more resilient it is to change and stress, and the more opportunities it provides for continuity in the face of change, including global changes such as climate change and increased human activity.

If you want to interact with Alaska's wildlife, do it ethically so that we all stay safe and the animals are not harmed. Watching wildlife from a distance lets you see natural behavior without stressing or disrupting animals. Feeding animals, however well-intentioned, can change their foraging habits and make them dependent on food provided by humans.

Sudden flashes of light (from photographers) and loud noises can startle animals and cause them to flee or behave unnaturally. By keeping a respectful distance and minimizing disturbances, you can help to retain the integrity of these creatures' natural lives so that generations to come can also enjoy their presence.

You don't need to make grand gestures to support wildlife conservation – instead, think small, meaningful actions. Adopt an animal through a conservation program; these adoptions fund research and habitat protection.

Wildlife rehab centers are tirelessly nursing injured or orphaned animals back to health in order for them to be released back to the wild – donating to these centers or volunteering your time can make a big difference in their ability to continue this work. Advocacy is also a powerful tool. By supporting legislation that protects wildlife and their habitats, you help facilitate conservation work in the long term. Write to your local representatives about important issues, sign petitions, and spread the word. Every action, no matter how small, can support the larger effort to save Alaska's wildlife.

And there are success stories, which help motivate us. The bald eagle, on the brink of extinction from pesticides and habitat loss a few decades ago, is a good example. Populations of the iconic American bird rebounded when pesticides were outlawed and habitat was restored and protected. Artificial breeding programs for endangered animals are another good story.

In some cases, they've been a lifeline, keeping animals from going extinct. The management of such programs carefully considers factors such as which individuals are most likely to breed and how to manage matings in order to preserve genetic diversity. These efforts are important evidence that conservation work can make a difference.

Final Thoughts

It is everyone responsibility to ensure the continued health of ecosystems and the communities that rely on them. Preserving the future health of the landscapes that form the foundation of Alaska's wildlife, and the cultures that are tied to them. By interacting ethically, giving support, and advocating and celebrating successes, we help safeguard wildlife around the globe. As we turn this page, let's keep these lessons in mind. And let's keep our eyes open as stewards of the natural world, for we are in a position of responsibility and privilege.

Chapter Thirteen

Navigating Weather and Terrain

Standing on your cruise ship's deck, sailing through the icy waters of Alaska, the sun is shining brightly one minute, but that quickly changes. A few clouds roll in, it cools off, and starts to drizzle. Remember, it's Alaska. You get a taste of it all: sun, clouds, drizzle, and more. That's the nature of the weather there, and it's this inherent unpredictability that makes packing versatile clothing an art and a science.

Layering is your best friend when it comes to adapting to Alaska's fickle weather. It's a simple, effective idea: wear many layers of clothing all at once, then add or remove as conditions change. The first layer is the base layer, and it should wick or spread moisture away from your skin so that you stay dry.

Merino wool and polyester are great choices: they manage moisture well and still provide a bit of insulation. Next comes the middle layer, which is all about heat. Go for fleece or synthetic insulation here, as these materials will retain your body heat as you hike. Finally, there's the top layer, your shield against wind and rain.

Here's where a good waterproof jacket comes in handy. A well-made jacket will keep you out of the elements and still let your body breathe. Adjusting these layers throughout the day will allow you to be comfortable whether you're hiking through a sun-drenched meadow or caught in a sudden downpour.

Warm hats and gloves are essential, especially in the early morning 'magic hour' and later at night when it can get quite chilly even in the summer. Sunglasses with UV protection are a must.

The sunlight reflecting off the snow and water is extremely bright, and after a few hours squinting, your eyes are very sore. You get used to it, but glasses help prevent it.

Quick-drying towels are also useful (I always take two) to dry off after a dip in a glacial lake and a quick wipe over my face and hands if it starts to pour. The large plastic ones are fine, but the quick-drying cotton ones are best. These are all the little things that make a huge difference for comfort and being ready for any kind of weather in Alaska.

Multi-use gear eliminates the need for specific items and can reduce your drag dramatically. Zipper-off convertible pants allow you to adapt to changes in temperature mid-day. An all-season packable rain jacket can be stashed in a daypack when not in use, but instantly deployed at the first sprinkle. Multi-purpose items such as these enable you to pack and travel lighter with fewer items, while still being well-equipped and comfortable.

To be tech-savvy is to have the right item and accessories all the time—especially in Alaska, where weather is quite unpredictable at times. A waterproof phone case is always a wise investment. It's good to have your phone always protected from the unpredictable elements, and also to take pictures freely without the anxious thought that your phone might get damaged because of the rain. A portable weather radio is always helpful, especially in isolated places where cell services might be very inconsistent. It helps one be warned of any impending weather changes, and can give you ample time to prepare or adjust your plans if the predicted weather conditions turn out to be severe.

Packing Checklist

- **Layers of clothing**: merino wool or polyester base layers, insulating fleece or synthetic jackets, waterproof shells.

- **Accessories**: warm hats, gloves, UV-protection sunglasses, quick-drying towels.

- **Multi-Purpose Gear**: Convertible pants, lightweight rain jackets.

- **Tech Gadgets**: Waterproof phone case, portable weather radio.

This list will leave you well-prepared for the fickle nature of Alaskan weather so that you can enjoy all of the wonders that await you, rather than worrying about specific details. If you're prepared to be affected, you'll be ready for anything that nature throws your way.

Adapting Your Itinerary to Weather Changes

Weather in Alaska can be as unpredictable as it is beautiful. Spring can yield clear, sunny days one moment, and then it can pour with rain or arrive with sudden fog the next. Having a flexible schedule is a great way to turn potential travel disruptions into new opportunities. Built-in buffer days are a smart move.

They act as a cushion, allowing for postponement of weather-related delays without throwing the entire itinerary into chaos. The extra days can be used to revisit favorite destinations, explore new areas, or kick back and relax. Back up, indoor-friendly activities are a great way to fill your time in case the plan was to spend the day outside. A local museum, a café, or a cultural event are great ideas. Not only do they help you stay dry—they reveal more about the Alaskan heritage.

Knowing the current weather and what conditions are in store before heading out can be key to making the most of your trip. And, as with many things in life, technology can give you a leg up. Having a weather app on your phone is indispensable—and having one that will alert you to severe weather in your vicinity is downright crucial.

These apps often have real-time warnings that enable you to get ahead of the curve and know when you might have to change plans. Some of these apps will even provide more detailed forecasts or the best times to experience certain outdoor activities based on the current weather patterns.

Another good idea is to check in with a local tourism office; they often have the most relevant information about the local weather—including any surprises—and how to get around that without having to scrap your entire itinerary. In addition to the standard information you'll find on their websites, they might have insider tips for how to get around those weather bumps, including touristy things to do that might be less affected by the weather, or are less well-known to those who haven't been to that region before.

Sometimes, even with a great itinerary, activities get rescheduled due to unpredictable weather. Being flexible and proactive about rescheduling can make a big difference. Typically, it's quite easy to contact tour operators for rescheduled dates.

Virtually all reputable operators are accustomed to the vagaries of the Alaskan weather, and will do their best to reschedule when they can. Make sure to ask your tour providers about contingency plans, so you can be aware of the options ahead of time. Plan to explore seasonal indoor activities. Many areas have fascinating indoor venues such as aquariums, art galleries, or cultural centers, which offer enriching experiences, regardless of what is happening outside.

You can handle minor changes in weather gracefully if you stay in contact with your guides and tour operators. Keeping in touch with the people you're traveling with ensures you are aware of any changes in schedule.

You can also sign up for text alerts from tour companies that will let you know if the schedule changes or possibly if your tour is canceled. This can help you not worry about whether you will be informed of a change. It's also useful to check the cancellation policies and fees up front before you book your trip.

This might help you to frame your expectations for the trip, and know what to expect if you need to alter your plans. If you have a good understanding of the flexibility promised by the booking terms, you're going to feel much less panic about what to do next.

Learning to accommodate Alaska's fickle weather is a matter of being flexible and having options ready to roll in case of change. It is an approach that turns a 'problem' into a discovery, a challenge, and an opportunity. Use buffer days, take advantage of technology, and communicate, and your Alaskan experience will be as satisfying as you hoped, whatever the skies deliver.

Safely Exploring Remote Terrains

The wilderness is beautiful, but we have to respect it—you can't take on Alaska's wild places without preparation and respect for the land. It is big and beautiful, and often dangerous. There's wilderness, and then there is wilderness…

The prep starts with basics: a good map and a good compass. These are your true friends when you're in landscapes where even seasoned adventurers can easily get lost. A GPS device is helpful, but it can fail in weak-signal areas. Reading a map and using a compass allows you to get back to safety.

Secondly, have an extra food and water supply. The sheer size of Alaska means that a hike quickly becomes an all-day journey, and enough provisions mean a small snafu doesn't become a major problem. High-energy food such as nuts and granola bars, plus water purification tablets, are your safety net if you end up changing your plans.

Traveling in a group is safer than going it alone—and it's more fun. You can divide up the tasks of navigation, taking some of the pressure off each individual. Take turns leading and looking at the map to make sure that you're all staying on track and oriented.

Group check-ins and emergency plans will only make things feel safer. Agree on regular check-in points before setting off from the start of your route. Agree on what you will do if someone gets separated. This planning will make you feel safer—and also, if the worst happens, you'll be ready to deal with it.

Another essential consideration is being well-equipped with the right emergency protocols and tools. A satellite phone and personal locator beacon (PLB) are essential in regions with no cell coverage.

A satellite phone allows you to make a phone call to the outside world, and, if needed, a PLB can send a distress signal to the rescue services. It might seem like overkill, but these devices could in fact mean the difference between life and death. It is also important to have basic knowledge of first aid and survival.

Being able to treat minor injuries such as cuts or sprains will prevent those accidents from blowing up into something much bigger. Survival skills such as learning how to build a simple shelter or start a fire will ensure your comfort and safety should you find yourself unexpectedly spending a night outdoors.

The wild backcountry is like a siren's call to explorers from all over the world. Adventurers want to visit Alaska's most remote places to experience its wilderness for what it truly is. Being prepared and remaining respectful to the environment are crucial aspects of any trip. Every step into the backcountry is a step into the unknown, but with the right mindset and gear, it can be an adventure that rewards you for trying.

Understanding Alaskan Altitudes and Health Tips

Many of Alaska's best places to go wild are at higher elevations, where the air is thinner, and the landscape is wilder. But these altitudes can also be surprising—and sometimes challenging—for those not used to them. Altitude does strange things to the body, and being aware of these changes can help keep your adventure safe and enjoyable. At high altitude, low oxygen levels can lead to altitude sickness: dizziness, nausea, and headaches are common. It's your body's early warning system, signaling that it is trying to adjust to an environment of lower oxygen availability.

If you feel these early symptoms, you need to respond and try to avoid it getting worse. Thinner air also affects hydration and stamina. You might feel more fatigued, and you'll need to stay hydrated, since the body loses moisture more easily at altitude.

The best way to accustom yourself to higher altitude and minimize health risks is by climbing gradually. This means hiking up only so many thousands of feet a day, rather than making a sharp ascent of several thousand feet in one go.

This way, your body has time to adjust as you gain elevation, minimizing the risk of altitude sickness. Hydration is important—drinking more water than you usually do to help your body cope with the dry, earthy mountain air and as a general marker of good health. Rest is important too. This means getting as much sleep as you need and, while you rise, taking breaks when you're walking or exercising. The combination of hydration, rest, and gradual exposure can make all the difference to how well you feel and perform as you ascend.

The mountains of Alaska are beautiful and certainly have their allure, but don't let them fool you. High altitude comes with health risks. The lower oxygen available at altitude will likely make you feel short of breath. Practice breathing to help you deal with this.

Slow, deep breaths can help increase oxygen intake and decrease breathlessness. Reducing your alcohol and caffeine consumption will also help. Both of these can worsen dehydration, which works to magnify altitude symptoms. Reducing these can help your body acclimatize and ensure you are feeling your absolute best while you are out there adventuring.

If you are planning an activity at high altitude, a pre-trip medical evaluation is a good idea. Your physician can identify any personal health risks and help you plan so that you can best manage the effects of altitude. Your doctor may prescribe certain medications to prevent altitude sickness, such as acetazolamide, which makes your body adapt to altitude better and avoid some of the symptoms. These consultations offer reassurance, and give you the knowledge and tools to tackle the challenges of higher elevation.

Final Thoughts

Alaska's landscapes are incredible—but they come with potential hazards. Armed with the knowledge of what altitude can do, you can now grasp what it takes to minimize these effects on your body and your journey. With the right mindset and precautions, Alaska's heights become another facet of your experience, one for you to savor and enjoy.

Chapter Fourteen

Transportation and Logistics Simplified

You're in a small plane, crisscrossing the vast wilderness of Alaska. Look down from the cockpit window and you see a patchwork of jagged peaks, green forests, and braided rivers weaving through the landscape.

This is the world through the windows of a bush plane or a floatplane. And it's an altogether different experience than looking at Alaska from the window seat of a commercial airliner. Bush planes and floatplanes are not just a fun way to travel: they are the only way to get to many places. Over Denali National Park or landing on a remote alpine lake, bush planes and floatplanes open up a world that cannot be reached by road.

The workhorse of the fleet is the bush plane, revered for its durability and utility. Bush planes fly routes that connect small communities to big-game hunters and adventurers to remote Alaska lodges and outposts.

Maybe you fly over the Brooks Range where thousand-foot hills stretch to the horizon. Perhaps you fly to the Arctic Circle where endless tundra and meandering rivers dominate the landscape. These routes are about the journey as much as they are about the destination, and the overhead views are unparalleled.

Floatplanes are a breed apart. These planes take off and land on water, offering a different type of adventure. Imagine flying over a remote lake as the plane skims across the water's mirror-smooth surface, surrounded by peaks and forests.

Booking a flight on a bush plane or floatplane is pretty easy, though there are a few things to think about. It is good to plan ahead if possible, particularly during the heavy tourist season, as these flights can sell out. Many of the operators have online booking, which makes reserving a flight simple.

You will usually get a pre-flight briefing that will cover safety protocols and give a general overview of the planned journey. This is a good time to ask questions or get details about what to expect. Most visitors to Alaska take a flightseeing tour over Denali, North America's tallest peak. Some people will do nothing more than that, but flights to remote lodges, accessible only by air, take you deeper into the wilderness than virtually any road can.

The operators of these bush planes and floatplanes are safety-conscious, and there is a high degree of safety regulation. The Federal Aviation Administration (FAA) regulates the flying of private aircraft, and regular maintenance checks are required; aircraft must pass safety requirements. Before you fly, the pilot briefs you on safety and emergency procedures, and shows you the various features of the aircraft. With such stringent safety rules, you are free to relax and enjoy the experience.

One of the highlights of an Alaska trip for many travelers is flying in a small plane over the wilderness. Seeing a herd of caribou on the tundra below, or a grizzly bear catching a salmon in a river: these are memories you carry away with you, and stories to tell afterwards.

What's a new, thrilling experience you've had? Describe it, and what emotions and thoughts you had during it. How did it alter your perspective of something, or bring you closer to something? Thinking about such moments can make your travel experience richer, and can make you more open to the adventure that awaits you in Alaska.

Efficiently Scheduling Your Alaskan Journey

When you plan an Alaskan trip, making a thorough itinerary becomes more than a good idea; it's a necessity if you hope to see as much of the state as possible. Start by crafting a master itinerary, including buffer times.

This boils down to padding your schedule, creating wiggle room if there's a delay or some other outside factor that throws your plans off. What the buffer times do is provide space to breathe, which can turn potential stress into unexpected new discoveries that make the trip feel more organic and less like a tick-box exercise.

Prioritize sights: it's easy to feel overwhelmed by what to see and do when you have so many options and so little time. Decide which sights or experiences matter the most to you: is it Denali? The coastal fjords? Anchorage's cultural heft? Build your schedule around your key experiences.

Coordinating times across multiple forms of transport can seem daunting, but with the right tools this becomes much more manageable. Travel apps that offer real-time updates on weather, traffic, and disruption can be invaluable here, as can keeping an eye on your flight times and your hotel reservations.

These tools really help your finger stay on the pulse of your trip, so you can shift and adapt when necessary. Also, make sure to schedule in some downtime for rest and exploration. Alaska is best appreciated slowly, where you can just take in the surroundings without feeling like you have to rush off to the next place. It could be something as simple as an afternoon in the local café, or a stroll through one of the many national parks to soak up the atmosphere of the area. These can end up being the highlights of your trip.

One of the best ways to be thrifty is to book your transport and accommodation in advance. Not only will you save money—many tour operators and hostels offer early bird and package deals—but you'll know that you will always have a roof over your head and a bed to sleep in.

Many tour operators and hostels operate on a first-come, first-serve basis, so the sooner you reserve, the better your chances of getting exactly what you want. Plus, using reservation systems for tours and accommodation is a great way of getting discounted rates and extra perks. Knowing where you're staying and that your transport is booked is a great feeling when you're on the road, allowing you to focus less on logistics and more on enjoying the adventure.

A schedule can always have a glitch or two, so one way to avoid disaster is to have some flexibility in your tickets for transportation. If you have open-dated tickets, you can change dates or times without a substantial fee. If itinerary changes do occur, you can keep your service providers involved in the conversation so that they can help you with your changes.

Many companies are more forgiving if you keep them in the loop, and they might have an alternative they can offer you or even be able to reschedule. This way, if something small goes wrong it doesn't derail your Alaska trip.

Navigating Alaskan Railways and Ferries

Imagine the scene: you're snug with a window seat, watching Alaska roll by—its great mountain passes, its deep-green forests, its rivers, and its lakes. You're on the Alaska Railroad, which has been ferrying people across the state since the early 20th century. The destination might be Fairbanks, or perhaps Anchorage, but the Alaska Railroad takes you directly through the heart of the state, offering a window into all that it holds.

From the comfort of your seat, you can pass through several distinct biomes, from the temperate rainforests near the coast to the subarctic tundra of the interior. From Alaska's state capital to its largest city, you'll ride past the state's most famous natural landmark, Denali. You might eat your lunch in the shadow of the great mountain.

Alaska is a vast state, so much larger than the contiguous 48, that it can be a challenge to travel through. The ferries are unreliable, the roads sparse, and the distances vast. There are few places on the planet where a train plays such a crucial role in the movement of people, but that's the case in Alaska, where the railroad can take you exactly where you want to go.

If you ride along the Denali Star from Anchorage to Fairbanks, you'll see the Susitna River, its still water reflecting the majestic Mt Denali; you'll pass the peaks of the Chugach Mountains. When you gaze out the window at the majestic Denali, you can't help but wonder at the scale of the land around you. If you take the Coastal Classic from Anchorage to Seward, you will pass through the Kenai Peninsula, where Sitka black-tailed deer and Dall sheep peer from the rocky cliffs, and where the bore tide pours its laden waters into Turnagain Arm.

Getting there requires another shift, from rail to sea, as visitors to Alaska can experience by traveling on the coastal ferries of the state-owned system known as the Alaska Marine Highway System. it's a continuous link that connects the coastal communities, allowing travelers a chance to experience and participate in Alaska's maritime diversity.

The ferries, for example, run from Bellingham, Washington through the Inside Passage to the Aleutian Islands, or make island-to-island hops in Southeast Alaska. Sailing from one place to another is a slow, intimate way of exploring.

It means looking at the coast from a different perspective—one where the horizon is long, and the rhythm of the sea is echoed by the motion of the ship. Picture sailing past rugged cliffs and watching pods of whales breaching in the distance. Island-hopping in Southeast Alaska means uncovering a string of small towns filled with history and charm. The people are as friendly as the scenery.

It pays to book your rail and ferry tickets ahead of time, especially during the high-traffic summer months. Not only does booking ahead guarantee your spot, but you can save money by booking in advance.

When booking your rail trip, consider the classes of service available. If you're on the Alaska Railroad's GoldStar Service, you have a glass-domed ceiling to maximize your views and get every detail of the passing scenery. On the ferries, you can book private cabins or just relax in the solariums. The online booking systems make it easy to plan your trip in advance, and many operators are becoming more flexible, allowing changes if your plans change.

Onboard, take advantage of the experiences available: many trains and ferries offer onboard dining with locally sourced Alaskan cuisine as rich and diverse as the landscapes traversed. Enjoy seafood that was caught fresh that morning or a meal that fuels your day's activities.

Many services offer educational programs and talks about the natural and cultural history of the regions traveled through. These programs offer a deeper understanding and appreciation of Alaska, which can be enriching for passengers. As you sit down in your cabin, let the rhythm of the rails or the gentle rocking of the ship become part of your experience of Alaska. Every moment spent onboard can be an opportunity to connect with the land and sea.

The Role of Cruise Ships in Alaskan Travel

Cruise ships are the lifeblood of Alaska tourism. Last year, 1.2 million people came to the state by cruise. Part of the draw is the chance to access landscapes and communities unreachable by car. Some of the largest cruise companies—Princess Cruises, Holland America Line, and Royal Caribbean—run itineraries through the Inside Passage and Gulf of Alaska.

Each offers a unique margin of experience: Princess Cruises' "Crown Jewel" itinerary focuses on Alaska's glaciers, whales, and bears; Holland America's "Alaska's Glacier Country Cruise" is perfect for exploring Southeast Alaska's majestic, wildlife-rich Inside Passage; and Royal Caribbean's "Alaska Inside Passage" offers a 10-day tour including an overnight in Victoria, British Columbia.

A cruise is the perfect way to see a lot of Alaska without the hassle of unpacking and repacking. You wake up in your room watching a glacier pass by, scale a glacier, float in a kayak, or fly in a helicopter. Alternatively, you might lounge with a view of the water or gaze out the window of your balcony while sipping coffee. It's easy to see why so many people choose to travel to Alaska this way.

Cruise travel brings huge economic benefits to these communities. In towns such as Juneau, Ketchikan, and Sitka, locals are eager to serve the demand of arriving visitors. Tour operators, artisans, restaurateurs, and craft enterprises thrive on the demand created by cruising. Local businesses, bars, and restaurants see new customers daily, and employees gain jobs and livelihoods.

Many cruisers come to Alaska with a desire to experience something different, and they often participate in guided tours and cultural experiences that showcase local traditions. For local entrepreneurs, cruise visitors present a prime opportunity to showcase their offerings during the summer season.

Cruise tourism generates significant economic benefits. A 2011 University of Alaska report documented $308 million in cruise spending in 2010. In Juneau, 90% of cruise passengers spend money onshore. However, the question remains: can this economic benefit be reconciled with the cultural and environmental character of these communities, allowing for sustainable growth?

The biggest selling point of cruise ships for travelers is their all-inclusive, hassle-free nature. Accommodations, meals, and entertainment are packaged together. Onboard, travelers have a wealth of activities to choose from, including live shows, lectures, fitness centers, and pools. Cruises make it easy to visit multiple destinations in one trip, organized and convenient. Imagine cruising through Glacier Bay National Park, exploring the bustling streets of Skagway, and sipping hot cocoa while admiring the beauty of Tracy Arm Fjord—all on one trip.

However, the environmental impact of cruise ships is significant, raising concerns about emissions, waste, and the health of marine ecosystems. Many cruise lines are transitioning to cleaner fuel technologies such as liquefied natural gas, reducing reliance on heavy fuel oils.

Partnerships with conservation organizations are also increasing, allowing cruise lines to collaborate with experts and develop strategies to minimize their environmental footprint and promote responsible tourism. Ensuring Alaska's landscapes and waters remain pristine for future generations will require sustained efforts from the cruise industry and its travelers.

The right cruise for you depends on your interests, budget, and preferred experience. For wildlife, cultural visits, or scenic landscapes, review itineraries to find the best fit. Smaller ships or expedition cruises provide less crowded excursions, while larger ships offer more amenities, shopping, shows, and dining options.

Consider ship size, passenger capacity, and how these factors influence your desired experience. Do you want to see a pod of orcas or relax in a quiet cove? There's a cruise itinerary for nearly everyone who dreams of experiencing Alaska.

Final Thoughts

Choosing the right Alaskan cruise involves deciding what you want to see and how you want to explore. With so many options, from luxury to adventure or a mix of both, you can craft a trip that aligns with your vision. Whatever you choose, remember the journey is as important as the destination. Each moment aboard offers another chance to connect with Alaska's beauty and culture.

Chapter Fifteen

Photography and Capturing Memories

You're on the deck of your cruise ship, camera in hand, as the reds and oranges of the Alaskan sunset sparkle over the water. The foothills of the mountains grow long shadows, and if you don't capture this splendor, you're missing out on the experience.

You've got to get a picture, because in Alaska, every moment is a memory. But recording your experience isn't the same as capturing it. When you take that photograph, you're freezing the moment in time, and imprinting its beauty on you long after your trip is over.

Alaska is a photographer's dream. The rugged wilderness offers visual wonders around every turn. Whether you're an amateur or a professional, you're going to want to take pictures. The right equipment can help you preserve your visual memories.

Essential Photography Gear for Alaska

The variety of different landscape types in Alaska means that you'll need versatile camera equipment. Wide-angle lenses are particularly useful to capture large vistas, and they can make those majestic mountains and sprawling forests fit into one frame. For those instances where you want to show the full breadth of a sweeping landscape, a wide-angle lens is the perfect tool.

Meanwhile, if you happen to spot some wildlife, you'll be ready to zoom in – literally – with your telephoto lens. You may surprise a brown bear fishing in the stream or an eagle flying overhead. A telephoto lens lets you zoom in on these incredible creatures while you capture the details.

Accessories to take your outdoor photography to the next level are not to be overlooked. Firstly, you must have a tripod; you can't just ensure the stability of your camera by leaning it against a tree (it's actually against the law to disturb trees in a national park) or the side of your rental car, or anything else. Wind is often a factor in outdoor photography, and it's going to be moving your camera while you try to take that two-minute exposure of a waterfall or a night shot, unless you invest in a tripod.

You're also going to need a weatherproof camera bag. Alaska has unpredictable weather and you don't want your camera getting drenched in a sudden rainstorm. A good camera bag will keep everything safe and dry so that you can worry only about getting a good shot.

Moisture, especially, is an issue in Alaska's harsh environments, and silica gel packs are an easy way to fight it – keep your camera dry as humidity levels rise by storing it in a zip-loc bag with one of these little boxes. Another simple thing is to regularly give your lenses and sensors a good clean. Dust, moisture, and even pollen can degrade the quality of your images, so making sure your kit is spotless is important – having a cleaning kit on hand ensures that your camera is ready to go whenever a new vista presents itself.

If you don't want to miss an image because of a technical glitch, you'd better keep your gear in good order. Besides being an essential consideration for data security, technical backups are just as important as the photos themselves: there is nothing more frustrating than losing images because of a technical failure, so make sure you have safe, reliable backup solutions available.

If you want an easy, quick solution to back up your photos on the go, look no further than portable external hard drives. Many are small and rugged, and they can comfortably handle large files, making them the perfect choice for traveling. Cloud services provide a second tier of security, allowing you to upload your images from any location where you have access to the internet. As an added bonus, some cloud services even allow offline access, which allows you to store your images safely knowing that if you do lose your gear, your photos won't be lost with it.

Photography Preparation Checklist

- **Cameras and Lenses:** Wide-angle and telephoto lenses for versatility.
- **Tripods:** Essential for stability in varied weather conditions.
- **Camera Bags:** Weatherproof to protect gear from the elements.
- **Maintenance Tools:** Silica gel packs and cleaning kits to keep equipment in optimal condition.
- **Data Backup:** Portable hard drives and cloud storage for secure image preservation.

The checklist ensures that you are prepared to record everything you experience in Alaska: the sandy beaches and snow-covered mountain tops, the wildlife in its natural habitat. These tools are integral to the experience, serving a purpose as a medium to capture a place that might otherwise be lost to the winds of time.

Capturing the Northern Lights

Have you ever stood beneath an ethereal sky – flecked with greens and purples – that seemed to be putting on a show just for you? It's the Aurora Borealis, or Northern Lights, a natural phenomenon that draws photographers from all over to capture images of one of Earth's most spectacular light shows.

The Lights occur when charged particles, expelled by the Sun, collide with the Earth's atmosphere, breaking apart and causing light waves to dance across the sky. These illuminations are particularly vivid during times of high solar activity, called solar maximums.

The best time to view the show is between November and January, when nights are longest. In Alaska, because there is little light pollution, some of your best bets for viewing the Northern Lights can be found here.

The main issue with taking pictures of the Northern Lights is that your camera is lacking a bit of chromatic intelligence in comparison to what your eye can perceive. You'll have to open the aperture a bit more and play with other settings such as exposure time and ISO to lighten the shot and bring out some color that the naked eye might not see completely.

To start with, set your aperture to a longer exposure time, i.e., you'll open the shutter for a while to let in more light. In this case, we're going for something between 15 and 30 seconds. Next, lower your aperture to f/2.8 or f/4 to let in as much as possible. You'll want to keep your ISO high, between 800 and 1600, to catch the faintest of auroras.

Switch your lens to the manual focus setting and put it on infinity to make sure the stars and aurora are sharp. You'll be playing with exposure, ISO, and aperture settings, sometimes all at once, but don't be afraid – just keep practicing, and eventually you'll find the right balance for the conditions you're working with.

The challenge of aurora photography has as much to do with composition as the lights themselves. Composition in photography is about storytelling – capturing an image that tells a story. The frame is an opportunity to incorporate other elements of the landscape into your photos.

Consider the night sky beyond the aurora. If the rest of the sky is dark, then you might consider including silhouettes of trees or mountains in the foreground of your shot – or the reflection of the lights in a lake, even on a cold and clear winter's night. Placing silhouettes in the foreground of a long-exposure shot will bring depth to your image, as well as a sense of place and scale. Reflections in a body of water can also work well.

A calm lake can provide a mirror to the aurora, doubling the visual impact of the lights and adding a sense of symmetry to your image. Every image you create becomes a story, inviting the viewer to step into the scene, peer into the frame, and open their eyes to the wonder of the night sky.

You can stand outside on a cold night in Alaska, if you have the right gear and the right approach. Layer up. Start with a set of moisture-wicking base layers, then move up to some type of insulating layer (fleece or down), and finally finish with a windproof and waterproof outer shell.

Keep your extremities warm with some warm gloves and a hat. Nothing can cut a shoot short faster than getting cold so focus on your extremities. A thermos filled with a hot drink will add some comfort to those long exposure shots. Make sure you take some high-energy snacks, like some nuts or chocolate, to keep your energy up and your spirits high during the shoot. With the right gear and a little preparation, you can enjoy the experience of shooting the Northern Lights without freezing your butt off.

Techniques for Wildlife Photography

Seconds tick by as you, perched on a rock at the edge of a forest clearing, have your camera at the ready with the setting equivalent of a tripwire saying, 'Alaska's wildlife, DO NOT PASS GO.'

This is as much a game of patience as it is timing, for wildlife photography hinges on your ability to learn an animal's behavior. Animals are creatures of habit. Much of their day-to-day activity is tied to time of day.

Many species of animals are most active in the early mornings and late afternoons, which are known as 'peak activity times.' I learned to plan my shoots around these times. For example, I would set up to take pictures of a bear fishing at a stream at the edge of a clearing shortly after sunrise, or of a moose grazing in the open around golden hour. Learning the behavior of an animal will help you predict their movements. When you do, you become a master of timing yourself.

When it comes to wildlife photography, natural light is the most important tool you have, and knowing how to use it well is half the battle. The best time for shooting, or the golden hour, is just after sunrise and before sunset, when the soft warm light bathes the landscape, adding depth and richness to your photographs.

It's a great time to shoot animals, as the gentle glow of morning or evening picks up intricate little details such as the dusting of black on a silver fox's back or the delicate tones of a kingfisher's plumage. Wide-open midday light, on the other hand, creates strong contrasts and deep shadows that obscure detail, so it's best to avoid shooting at this time of day unless you have a shaded area or can use the light creatively. Let natural light gently pick out details and shimmering glints so that your subjects are engulfed in the soft glow of morning or evening.

Composition is the real intersection of creativity and technique, as it's what allows you to make interesting images that tell a story. You can make a photo more balanced and interesting by applying the rule of thirds, which you can think of as dividing up your frame into nine equal sections by two horizontal and two vertical lines.

If you place your subject on one of these lines or at one of the four intersections, the viewer's eye will be naturally drawn to that focal point. Panning is a technique where you track a moving subject with your camera and capture a sharp subject while the rest of the image is blurred. It takes a little practice to master, but it can lead to some interesting and dynamic photos.

There are ethics to think about here. You want to respect your subjects, keeping your distance if they are wild animals, so that your presence doesn't interfere with their natural behavior and doesn't put them at risk. Most experts recommend staying at least 100 feet away from large animals, such as bears and moose.

If you get too close, you also put yourself in danger. Flash photography can also disturb wildlife, startling animals with its bright light, causing undue stress. Use natural light and adjust the settings on your camera to accommodate available light levels so that you won't need to add artificial light to your photos. Trying to get as close as possible will ruin the photographs and scare the animals. If you want good photos, respect your subject; good photos contribute to the preservation of wildlife.

Every shutter-click in Alaska is an opportunity to preserve the wilderness, to make a picture of nature, a portrait of life in its purest form. With good timing, light, composition, ethics, and patience, your wildlife photography in Alaska can testify to the beauty and vulnerability of Alaska's primitive landscapes.

Creating a Visual Journey Through Your Lens

Imagine turning the pages of a photo book that details your trip to Alaska. Each spread is a chapter of the story, an image capturing a moment in time that speaks of more than just scenery – it tells of an experience, an emotion, a discovery. Using your photos to tell a story allows you to relive your trip, and share it with others, in a way that words alone can't.

Your camera is a storyteller, helping you document a series of events that, when sequenced together, form a visual narrative. Start with milestones: perhaps the first sight of a glacier, or the first laugh over a local dish. Add these images to your story – like chapters in a book, each one builds more depth and context into your experience.

Along the way, try to add to the story by photographing the local culture and customs you come across. Every area of Alaska has its own character, from the facial expressions of its people to the style of its buildings to the pace of its life.

Images of brightly colored native dance, the intricate patterns of native artwork, or a crowded market day will help you tell your story while also capturing the essence of where you've been. Your photographs help you remember and help others experience a place through your eyes.

When you then bring these images home, the next step is the post-processing. Here, basic adjustments can help you put more focus on the main features of your images, and bring back details that would otherwise be lost in the shadows or highlights.

You can also crop out what you don't want and crop into what is important. Then a light adjustment of colors can make your image pop. Nothing should be overdone, but a little boost in brightness, contrast, or saturation can help your images reflect the way the scene actually felt and looked.

Next, you might want to share your photographic journey – so, after editing, you could go back and put the images into a book or album. You could tell your story in a tangible form, each page a chapter, each image a paragraph, like a roadmap of your journey from beginning to end. You could also share your photographs on social media. Here the audience is broader – with other travelers, photography enthusiasts, giving your voice to a wider audience. Add captions, explain your stories, carry on your adventures with a photo book.

Sequencing and curation is the key to keeping your story coherent: group your images into folders, and tag them by place, event, or theme; label your images by date so it's easy to find a specific shot, and avoid losing gems in the shuffle.

Then, edit your sets so that they have a theme or focus. These can be as broad as the natural beauty of Alaska, or as specific as the cultural diversity of its people. When you give your images direction, they don't flounder – and neither will your audience. Not only will it be easier to share your story, but it will also let you revisit your adventure through the eyes of a storyteller.

In turning your photographs into stories, you pay tribute to your specific Alaskan adventure. Each of the images serves as a gateway to a moment in time, a window into the world as you saw it.

Final Thoughts

These narratives exist beyond the confines of a single trip, linking the splendor of the Last Frontier to the life you're living. Each time you embark on a new journey, whatever the destination, each time you click the shutter and capture a moment, you're telling a story and sharing a part of your experience with the world. Your adventures don't end when you put down the camera; you're only just beginning.

Chapter Sixteen

Preparing for Safety and Emergencies

You're standing at the edge of a steep expanse of wilderness, and the air is crisp, the view is broad, and you are about to have a good time. But not just a good time: to make it a great time, there's a last step that must be accomplished before lacing up the boots and putting on the pack. This is the step that turns a good adventure into a great time, a step so integral to the Alaska experience that they make it a way of life.

Safety Protocols for Adventure Activities

When you don the necessary safety gear, it's like an extra layer of confidence. Before you visit Alaska and immerse yourself in its high-stakes adventures, imagine preparing for a trek across a glacier, where crushing ice below your boots almost makes you forget you're walking on ice in the first place. It's humbling.

But a helmet and a harness aren't just accessories: they're the reason you're able to get out there. A helmet is necessary in case you take a fall, or if a loose piece of ice dislodges from above. The harness is to secure you in a crevasse. Similarly, if you're ziplining in the dense canopy, the harness is, of course, essential to safety, but so are the gloves that protect your hands as you're flying through the air. Each trip feels like an extra layer of confidence and allows you to focus on the adventure rather than the risks.

Keeping with guide directions is also vital. Guides aren't just there to show you the way; they are experts whose knowledge about where you are will improve your experience and keep you safe. If you're going on a glacier trek, a certified guide knows the ice and will keep you away from danger and, perhaps more importantly, from features that a non-expert might not know to avoid.

For ziplining, licensed operators will have inspected every line and every platform to make sure that it is safe to use, and will make sure you feel comfortable about using it. If you follow their instructions, you can enjoy your experience knowing you are in safe hands. The landscape that might have once looked daunting is now just a playground waiting for you to explore.

Assessing the safety of activity providers is another step that shouldn't be skipped. Research providers with a proven record before setting off. Read online reviews and testimonials from previous adventurers.

Few travel experiences give you a better understanding of the professionalism and safety practices of a provider than a first-hand account from an adventurer who experienced it. Ask detailed questions about their safety records and certifications. Reputable companies will be happy to explain their protocols and extol their commitment to safety. These are the people you want in charge of your adventure.

Personal responsibility is foundational to adventure safety. Knowing your limits and what works for your body and mind is crucial. When you're preparing to go out, assess your skill level honestly. If you are learning something new, do a beginner-friendly version first and work your way up as you feel more confident.

Be mindful of how you're feeling physically. For instance, if you're feeling unwell or just not yourself, it might be best to forgo a challenging activity that requires peak performance. It's up to you to stay safe and be aware of what's best for your body.

Think of something you want to do, but always seem to put off. Something a little adventurous – something you've heard of other people doing, or where you've caught a glimpse of it on TV, but never really figured out how to do for yourself. 'I want to try rock climbing. I'm not even sure I could do it, but it looks fun.'

Well, test yourself. Ask yourself: where are you right now? What's your skill level and overall state of physical fitness? What can you do, right now, to start getting yourself ready to do this thing? What training do you need? What gear? Who could teach you? Who could get you started? Look up the providers, the trainers, the gear. See what it takes. Write down an action plan. Not just so that you can do the thing someday, but so that you can reframe this pattern of thought.

Emergency Preparedness in Remote Areas

When you venture into Alaska's backcountry, you are entering another world. The landscape is rugged and beautiful, but it is also wild and unpredictable. A plan tailored to the landscape is your first layer of insurance against the unexpected. This plan begins by identifying risks and hazards.

For someone traveling in Alaska, that could be a change in the weather, an encounter with wildlife, or even something as seemingly innocuous as a sprained ankle. Once you can identify a risk, you can anticipate, avoid, and plan for it.

Second, establish a communication plan. Before you leave to go somewhere, tell someone your plans, including when you expect to be back and what route you will take. That way, if things don't turn out as planned, someone knows when and where to start looking for you. It might sound somewhat obvious, but communication is important. There is no lonely place on this planet if you have a plan.

Equip yourself with the right emergency supplies, and you won't be as miserable. As the saying goes, your kit is only as good as the things inside it. A first aid kit is a no-brainer, but it should be supplemented with items such as blister treatments, insect repellent, and altitude sickness medications.

You need these things, not just because they are nice to have, but because they are essential to the unique challenges of remote travel. Multi-tools are another must-have. Cutting, sawing, and opening cans – these tools do it all. Then there are fire starters, whether a lighter, waterproof matches, or magnesium striker. A fire can keep you warm, cook your dinner, or signal for help. These are the tools that will save you when you're miles and miles from home.

Communication becomes vital wherever there is patchy or no cellphone service, and here satellite phones come into their own. You can still call emergency services, whether that's a 911 operator or local authorities, and let them know if you're in trouble, wherever you might be. The same goes for loved ones. The same goes for GPS technology and personal locator beacons – once activated, search and rescue will know exactly where you are.

All of these things involve an initial outlay – there's no getting away from that – but they can mean the difference between a rescue and a body. The ability to call for help when you really need it makes them invaluable. And wherever you are, unless you truly are in the most remote place on Earth, you're never truly alone.

The most valuable skill you can develop for staying safe and prepared in Alaska's wilderness is situational awareness. Situational awareness can be simply defined as maintaining an awareness of your surroundings at all times. For me, this means constantly monitoring weather, because it can change quickly.

It also means keeping up-to-date on local wildlife activity, which can affect my plans if I know, for example, that bears are highly active, or that there's been a recent sighting in the area. Situational awareness tends to be proactive and preventative, which is always preferable to being reactive and trying to clean up the mess after the fact.

Go Bag Checklist

Your go bag needs to be stocked with:

- A flashlight with extra batteries.

- A mobile phone charger.

- A whistle.

- Food and water for at least 72 hours.

- High-calorie/high-energy snacks such as granola bars or nuts.

- A refillable water bottle and purification tablets.

- Lightweight, weather-appropriate clothing, especially layers that allow you to adjust to temperature changes.

- Personal items such as a rain jacket, bandana, and comfortable shoes.

A go bag means thinking ahead about what might happen out there.

Understanding and Handling Wildlife Encounters

When you step out into the wilds of Alaska, you're entering a place where nature is boss. Encounters with wildlife are frequent and certainly possible. Understanding animal behavior can be the difference between a peaceful viewing and a tense stand-off.

Bears, for instance, are often misunderstood. Knowing what to look for in their tracks and scat can alert you to their proximity. Bear tracks are large, toed, and clawed. Scat is varied; depending on their diet, it can include berries, seeds, or fur. Moose, for example, provide signals to tell you if they are feeling threatened.

Take note of their body language. If moose ears are laid back, you are likely to see raised hackles and a lowered head. They are giving you a 'back off' signal. Knowing their signals helps you approach animals with respect and caution. You can see their needs coming and avoid confrontations.

When you're watching animals in the wild, keep your distance. The unpredictability of wild creatures means that proximity can lead to unnecessary stress or aggression. Stay at least 300 feet from bears and 100 feet from moose. Use a zoom lens to get close to your subject from a distance – that way, you can get a perfect image without intruding on their habitat.

When you take a picture, remember that your shutter click is happening on their land. You should be as unobtrusive as possible so they can continue their behavior. You should be a part of the environment, a silent witness in their world.

Being prepared to respond appropriately will do more than just keep you safe: it will help you reduce human-wildlife conflicts. A curious or aggressive bear might be deterred by making noise. Bears, in general, avoid conflict with people, and loud noises often cause them to retreat.

Clap your hands or yell and, if you have one, use a whistle. If a moose charges, stand your ground. Many charges are bluffs, and retreating can trigger a real chase. Remaining still signals to the animal that you are not a threat. These behaviors might feel counterintuitive, but they can defuse a potentially dangerous situation. This all comes down to remaining calm, assessing the danger, and responding accordingly.

Wildlife safety is a group responsibility, not just an individual one. Teach your kids (and your companions) to respect wildlife. Wild animals aren't pets, and treating them as though they are can be fatal for the animals and/or their families.

Teach kids that they aren't allowed to approach wild animals or pick up anything that's not their own, including abandoned or dead animals. Let kids know that it is OK to be curious, but that curiosity must be kept within the safe boundaries you set. Teach them that they should remain still, quiet, and hidden when watching wild animals. Explain that they should never try to touch them or get too close; the animals need space.

Staying Healthy and Safe on Your Cruise

Think of yourself on a cruise ship, sailing on the open sea, with beautiful blue water on every side of you, as far as your eyes can see. It's the first week of your cruise, and you've settled into a routine of life at sea. Staying healthy is an important part of that routine, and it all begins with good hygiene practices.

Washing your hands frequently is one of the most important strategies for disease prevention on a cruise. If you have access to soap and water, scrub for at least 20 seconds. Hand sanitizers are a helpful alternative, especially when you're on the go, but they should be used in addition to, not instead of, a good wash.

When there are thousands of people in a contained environment, there's an increased risk of spreading germs. If an outbreak of gastrointestinal ailments like norovirus occurs, avoid areas crowded with other passengers. These simple interventions can help keep your cruise as healthy as it is fun.

Most of all, cruises should be fun, but the constant movement of the ocean often results in seasickness. Overcoming this common problem is often simply a matter of preparation. Medications such as antihistamines, which are available without a prescription, can help alleviate symptoms so that you can enjoy your window view without feeling queasy.

You might even prefer to try acupressure wristbands or natural remedies like ginger. Drinking water is important for land and sea alike, and you'll want to stay hydrated throughout the day. Balancing your nutrition is another small choice that adds up in a big way. Cruise ship food is notoriously delicious, but you can keep your energy up by including fruits, vegetables, and lean proteins as part of your regular meals.

Onboard safety briefings and drills are all about keeping you safe. While familiarity might breed boredom, the information provided during safety briefings can be life-saving when an emergency occurs. Learn where the life jackets and emergency exits are located.

Knowing these details can mitigate panic and confusion and help you make faster, safer decisions, should they become necessary. Pay attention to the crew's instructions. They are professionals, and their job is to keep you safe. Cruise safety training is not just a formality; it is designed to prepare you and keep you safe.

Communication with medical staff on board is also important so that you can receive advice or treatment for any concerns as soon as possible. On every cruise ship, there is a medical facility with personnel that can treat most minor complaints and advise on more serious ones. If you are feeling unwell, do not hesitate to visit the medical center.

Final Thoughts

If you report symptoms early, this can help prevent illness from spreading to others and will ensure that you receive optimal care. The staff there are there to help you, so should you need to consult them, it will very likely put your mind at rest. You can then relax and enjoy your cruise. Keeping an open channel of information with the medical team means that you are never truly alone when it comes to your health, even when you are hundreds of miles from shore.

Ensuring Safety & Accessibility in Alaskan Adventures

Safety is a priority for every traveler, and for those with mobility needs, medical conditions, or accessibility considerations, planning ahead ensures a smooth and enjoyable Alaskan experience.

Adventure Activities: Many adventure tour operators offer adaptive equipment and specialized guides for travelers with disabilities. Before booking excursions like glacier trekking or ziplining, check if the provider offers accessible alternatives, such as shorter routes, seated zipline harnesses, or modified equipment. Those with limited mobility may find that small-group tours or private guides provide a more accommodating experience.

Emergency Preparedness: If traveling with a chronic medical condition or mobility device, packing extra medications, a lightweight portable mobility aid, and a personal medical alert system can be essential. For those needing assistance devices like a CPAP machine or oxygen tanks, cruise lines and tour operators can arrange proper storage and power access if requested in advance.

Wildlife Encounters: Observing Alaska's incredible wildlife is possible from accessible platforms, boardwalks, and designated viewing areas. Instead of hiking deep into the backcountry, consider boat-based wildlife tours or accessible nature reserves with level trails. These options provide the same breathtaking encounters with moose, eagles, and bears—without strenuous physical exertion.

Cruise Ship Safety & Health: Modern cruise ships prioritize accessibility, offering mobility-friendly cabins, accessible dining venues, and onboard medical assistance. Passengers should inform the cruise line ahead of time about any mobility or medical needs, allowing crew members to assist with embarkation, disembarkation, and emergency preparedness.

By taking proactive steps and choosing excursions tailored to individual needs, every traveler—regardless of physical ability—can safely experience the awe-inspiring landscapes and adventures that make Alaska unforgettable.

Chapter Seventeen

Sailing Away

That's about it for this journey through Alaska, so before we close we should recap everything we've gone through. From preparing for your trip to Alaska and learning about its culture and history to experiencing its scenery, wildlife, and food, I hope this guide has been of use to you. This book can serve as your one-stop guide for first-timers to last-timers, for those who want to experience Alaska for the first time or for those who have been back many times before.

It is a simple idea, but its ambition is grand: to enable you to have the best and most memorable experience in Alaska possible. To get the most out of the cruise, no matter which cruise you take, to soak up the history of native cultures of Alaska, to stimulate the senses, and to show you the best the state has to offer.

When you put this book down, there are a few things worth remembering. Plan and be flexible: Alaska's weather is fickle, and a flexible itinerary and smart packing go a long way. Remember the cultural lessons, too: respect for local residents and their ways makes for richer travel and leaves a lighter footprint. And above all, have fun. Kayak through fjords. Look at wildlife from afar. Let your curiosity guide you.

But this is just the start. Let what you've learned here inform a deeper dive into whatever interests you, and see where it leads you. Alaska is full of discovery, and there is always, always more. Want to learn more about wildlife photography? Explore Zeglis's extensive collection of photographs on his website, or check out *To the High Country* (1996) and *Cold Country* (2004), his books of wildlife photography. Need a deeper dive into Alaskan history? Check out the 1995 documentary *Shadow of the Eagle* (2004) to learn more about the life and times of Ikatamiak, or read *Alaska's Historic Sites and Buildings Inventory* (1977) for a detailed list of many of Alaskans' most enduring structures.

I hope you take the lessons you've learned and start planning an Alaskan cruise or adventure of your own. Write up your experience and share it with others. Maybe you'll inspire someone to go see this part of the world firsthand. You'll be returning to a community of travelers who appreciate the beauty and challenges of Alaska.

Thank you for taking me along on this trip through the book's pages. Our mutual obsession with travel and new experiences is what ties us together, and I hope that the guide has been of some use in expanding your world view. And, most of all, thank you for taking Alaska on with me.

I would love to hear from you, whether it's to give me your feedback on a guide, or to share your own experiences. Your input is invaluable and helps me to improve future guides. You can find me on social media or on travel forums.

We'll leave you with a final aspirational note as you embark on your next adventure in Alaska. Go forth with a sense of anticipation and confidence knowing that you've prepared yourself well, and that there is much to behold and savor in a world that is just waiting to be encountered. Travel presents its fair share of challenges, but there are also countless moments of joy. Let these be the memories that inspire you to go out and see the world with your eyes and heart wide open. Bon voyage, and safe travels as you encounter a place that's unlike any you've ever seen.

Chapter Eighteen

Voices from the Voyage

Your Feedback Makes Waves!

Thank you for embarking on this journey through Alaska with me. From the stunning glaciers to the awe-inspiring wildlife, I hope this guide has helped you plan the adventure of a lifetime.

If you found this guide useful, inspiring, or simply fun to read, I'd be thrilled to hear your thoughts! Your review not only helps me grow but also helps future adventurers find the tools they need to make their Alaskan dreams come true.

How to Leave a Review

1. **Scan the QR code.**

2. **Fill in your review:** Share your experience—what you loved, what helped, or even what you'd like to see in future guides.

3. **Hit Submit**: Knowing your review will help me and countless others explore Alaska!

Thank you for helping me inspire travelers everywhere. Together, we're creating unforgettable journeys!

Bon Voyage,
Diana from Ocean Breeze Adventures

Check Out this Adventure, Hawaii!

H awaii Cruising and Adventure Guide. What's better than visiting one amazing island? How about all four on a floating city? Here is a glimpse of what this guide has to offer.

The sun was setting over the Pacific as our cruise ship gently glided into the port of Maui. The air was filled with the scent of plumeria and saltwater, a welcome greeting after days at sea. I remember standing on the deck, watching as the island's lush green mountains came into view. The excitement among the passengers was palpable. We had just a single day to explore, and the possibilities seemed endless yet daunting.

This book is designed to capture that very essence of excitement and discovery. It aims to be your go-to guide for cruising Hawaii, whether you're a couple seeking romance, a family looking for fun, or someone needing wheelchair accommodations. With most cruise ships docking for only one to two days at each island, this guide focuses on making the most of your limited time.

Now, let me introduce myself. I am your guide, the number one best-selling author of Hawaii travel guides. Over the years, I've explored every nook and cranny of these beautiful islands. I've hiked its volcanic trails, swum in its azure waters, and delved deep into its rich culture and history. My extensive experience and profound love for Hawaii have equipped me with the knowledge to offer you the most enriching and authentic experiences.

What sets this guide apart is its practicality and inclusiveness. Traditional travel guides often have extensive itineraries that don't fit the tight schedules of cruise passengers. This book provides concise, actionable plans tailored to the 1-2 day port stops typical of most Hawaiian cruises. Additionally, it includes vital information for travelers with special needs, ensuring that everyone can enjoy the magic of Hawaii.

The structure of this book is straightforward and user-friendly. Each chapter focuses on a specific island, starting with an overview and moving into detailed itineraries. You'll find planning tips, cultural insights, and practical advice to help you navigate each port. Whether you're visiting Oahu's bustling Honolulu or the serene beaches of Kauai, you'll have everything you need to make informed decisions.

This guide is targeted at adults, including couples, families, and travelers with special needs. It caters to both first-time visitors and seasoned travelers looking for new experiences. Whether you're planning a honeymoon, a family vacation, or a solo adventure, this book has something for you.

You can expect actionable insights and tips throughout the book. From the best spots to catch a sunrise to must-visit local eateries, this guide is packed with insider knowledge. You'll learn how to avoid tourist traps, find hidden gems, and make the most of your limited time in each port.

As you turn the pages, I hope to inspire you with visions of the ultimate Hawaiian adventure. Picture yourself snorkeling in the crystal-clear waters of Molokini Crater, hiking the otherworldly landscapes of Haleakalā, or simply enjoying a traditional Hawaiian luau under the stars. This book is your ticket to an unforgettable journey, filled with thrilling activities, breathtaking beauty, and rich cultural experiences.

So, dear reader, I invite you to dive into this guide and start planning your Hawaiian adventure. Whether it's your first visit or your tenth, there's always something new to discover in Hawaii. Let's make the most of your cruise and create memories that will last a lifetime.

Aloha, Ocean Breeze Adventures.

Scan this code for a shortcut to my book on Amazon!

Praise for Ocean Breeze Adventures

Maui Travel and Adventure Guide—*2024 International Impact Book Awards winner*

Maui: Packed with amazing tips and insights, "Maui Travel and Adventure Guide: The Ultimate Shortcut to Thrills, Beauty, Culture, and Authentic Experiences" by Ocean Breeze Adventures is one book that will help any traveler plan their Maui adventure right from the very pages of this guide. This book has quite a few sections broken down into the different areas that make up the island region. Once the traveler picks the area they want to explore, they can read all the valuable information that area has to offer them such as places to stay, restaurants to eat in, hikes to go on, and types of tours to join in, etc. This is one travel guide this reviewer wanted to read to find out all the special nuances Maui offers travelers. The details listed, with the different locations of Maui, were informative and without a doubt, even if you have never been to this destination, Ocean Breeze Adventures takes all the guess work out of planning a beautiful, fun-filled vacation that your whole family will enjoy from start to finish. One adventure that sounds quite intriguing is the Mystery Maui excursion. It's a thrilling interactive adventure in which you journey through the island's mysteries and legends by solving puzzles, looking for clues, and discovering secrets along the way. This sounds like such a unique adventure. What vacationer wouldn't want to go and see the mysteries Maui has to offer them? Diana Freel is the mastermind behind her company, Ocean Breeze Adventures. She is an avid traveler and has come to realize that not every traveler has the time to thoroughly research the area they choose to vacation in. So, she decided to create travel and adventure guides to take the stress out of doing all the research yourself. Her book will present any traveler with all the information they might need in one handy guide. Interestingly enough, Ms. Freel is not only an author of travel guides but also audiobooks, coloring books for kids, and books on gardening, and has even penned two mystery books that will be available for readers to buy very soon. "Maui Travel and Adventure Guide" by Ocean Breeze Adventures has extensively researched Maui and documented what travelers need to know about this beautiful destination. She takes all the guesswork out of planning an enjoyable vacation to Maui. If you're planning a trip to Maui, consider reading this well-written travel guide. It comes highly recommended! Well done, Ms. Freel! – *ReaderViews.com*

Big Island: Bursting with insider tips and curated itineraries, this guide is a treasure trove for adventurers ready to dive into Hawaii's stunning landscapes and rich culture. From hidden waterfalls and dramatic lava tubes to vibrant beaches and ancient Hawaiian sites, every page sparks excitement for exploration. Say goodbye to travel stress and hello to unforgettable experiences! Whether you're hunting for the best snorkeling spots or seeking budget-friendly tips, this guide transforms your dream trip into an exhilarating reality! —*NewInBooks.com*

Also by Ocean Breeze Adventures

Scan this QR for a shortcut to all her guides on Amazon!

The books are also available on Audible and her website, www.oceanbreezeadventures.net!

Coming soon!

- From Glaciers to to Volcanoes Alaska and Hawaii Cruising and Adventure Guide Bundle

- Belize Travel and Adventure Guide

The perfect companion for any travel planning, my Travel Journal is the perfect place to plan, explore, experience, and capture the ultimate adventure.

Simply scan the QR code to access your copy directly on Amazon.

About Ocean Breeze Adventures

Diana Freel—writer, adventurer, and the proud founder of **Freel Publishing LLC and** the **Ocean Breeze Adventures Travel Agency**—has dedicated her life to two powerful passions: travel and storytelling.

Winner of the **International Book Impact Award** for her *Maui Travel and Adventure Guide*, Diana's love for exploration began the moment she could travel freely, documenting her adventures in journals as she roamed the world. But her journey hasn't been without challenges. In the late 90s, Diana faced unimaginable adversity, finding herself trapped in an abusive relationship and enduring the heartbreaking loss of her son in the most devastating of circumstances. After years of survival, she reached a turning point—determined to reclaim her life, she set out to find purpose and healing beyond her pain.

For Diana, travel became a source of renewal. Each destination offered a chance to breathe, connect, and rediscover freedom. With every journey, she uncovered a new sense of purpose, leading her to establish Freel Publishing LLC and Ocean Breeze Adventures. Now, as the owner of **Ocean Breeze Adventures Travel Agency**, Diana combines her passion for storytelling with personalized travel planning, helping others experience the world with ease and meaning.

Through her guides and agency, Diana empowers adventurers to embrace life's beauty, whether they're exploring the hidden gems of Hawaii, the rugged landscapes of Alaska, or other tropical destinations. Her mission is simple yet profound: to make travel transformative, accessible, and full of joy for everyone—especially those who seek a path to healing and new horizons.

Whether you're a survivor finding strength through travel or simply someone ready to embark on your next great adventure, Diana invites you to join her. The world isn't just a destination—it's a story waiting to be lived, and she's here to help you write yours.

Whether you're a survivor seeking new horizons or a curious soul ready for your next adventure, Diana invites you to join her. The world is more than a destination—it's a story waiting to be lived, and she's here to help you write yours.

Your Travel Advisor

You don't have to let planning for your once-in-a-lifetime trip deter you from going. I would be honored to help you plan your trip. To book a free 15-minute phone call with me, scan or click the QR code below.

Happy Adventures,

Diana at Ocean Breeze Adventures—Where Sand and Beauty Meets Adventure.

Made in the USA
Columbia, SC
01 July 2025